1

All rights reserved

All rights reserved. No part of this publication may be reproduced, stored or transmitted in any form or by any means, electronic, mechanical, photocopying, recording, scanning, or otherwise without written permission from the publisher. It is illegal to copy this book, post it to a website, or distribute it by any other means without permission.

Chi Jade Tran asserts the moral right to be identified as the author of this work.

Designations used by companies to distinguish their products are often claimed as trademarks. All brand names and product names used in this book and on its cover are trade names, service marks, trademarks and registered trademarks of their respective owners. The publishers and the book are not associated with any product or vendor mentioned in this book. None of the companies referenced within the book have endorsed the book.

Author's Wish

The book was based on a true story, however, a few facts remain relative as they could be seen from various angles by different characters, and the author wishes to reserve the best respect for each mentioned character in this book.

Preface

The book is a moving story about a young girl growing up in Vietnam during challenging times of her life. It shows us her journey and how her family's past, especially her bond with her grandfather, influences her life.

The story brings together her own experiences and those of her relatives and ancestors. The difficulties faced by her family, passed down from her grandfather to her dad, create an intermingled complex background for her own story.

What's striking about this book is its honesty. The author manages to talk about her family's painful past while keeping the pure and open viewpoint of a young girl.

When you read her book, you really get inside the main character's head. You see her world, where the tough times and the brighter moments exist side by side.

Reading this book, you really feel for the young girl. It makes you wish you could be there for her, in those moments of solitude under the calm night sky of Vietnam.

The book is a powerful reminder of how a well-told story can make readers feel a deep connection with the characters. The story also demonstrates the intricacies and distinctiveness of our minds and relationships. It gives us an insight into how a child can see her ancestors in a new light as she grows up. This book is a beam of light through time, right into the soul of a little girl and her view of the world and a sweet greeting to her late grandfather.

From a Reader

Contents

I. "It was the best of times, it was the worst of times..." 10

II. Strange is also a feeling..19

III. Between the city of bridges and the city where Saigon river flows..39

IV. What happened in Saigon? - Part One............60

V. This time I could tell you about that escapism..74

VI. The working and freedom Tale........................94

VII. What happened in Saigon? - Part Two.......107

VIII. Then the darkness monster came................120

IX. The handwritten letters.....................................135

X. Like a movie but not a destiny..........................145

XI. Those last summer days...................................165

XII. The sleepless nights..180

XIII. Back to Hue province......................................187

Short Story

The Well... 195

Ba */ba:/ father called in central Vietnam.*

my mother was
the first country
the first place I ever lived.
2016

I.

"It was the best of times,
it was the worst of times..."

Just a few months after my grandfather's funeral, I graduated from high school, passed the university entrance exam, and started the first college semester of my freshman year. Despite the seemingly acceptable status quo, a resurgent complex chain of emotions began to take over me during the same summer. Also in that year, I met and broke my first love. Was it a coincidence that these events keep on following one another? I did not know then and still, I do not know now.

Not for less than one time have I asked myself why and started to look for better answers. By writing down my thoughts, I figure that it may help. Notwithstanding I have to concede that one has got herself in inevitable dilemmas, one is supposed to see life as a much more delicate riddle by learning not to answer questions that ultimately do not serve.

Somewhere from the deeply balanced mien of a writer, I do not have much expectation except a little hope for a better world. It was an insightful journey, and it is now much more meaningful when I decide to take off the inveterate inner shyness to write it all down, my past.

I wrote these lines at the airport back in Vietnam after three and a half years of living in Spain. The air, the people, the accent and the manner of Vietnamese, the customs, and current trends, all blend into each other and dial into my sense of being. It completes my emptiness in an unexplainable way. Walking along Le Thanh Ton street in Saigon and the vicinity, striding from this corner of memory to the next one, resonates such a tranquil reflection that quickly vapors in the typical humid in the South of Vietnam.

Writing in Nam always brings me such a magical flow of ideas and inspiration. The tropical air blends in turbulent streets where lined-up stores are stacked with topsy-turvy merchandise, or even "half-a-store" businesses happened where different vendors may take their turn throughout the day and night to share monthly rent. Everything is open, and anything can happen. Yet after the "magical hours", somehow you could not open *that* door again. There would not be any more dancing and hopeless romance, no more of one's "lost shoe" left on the staircase of the royal castle. Everything was known, scripted, and even planned.

I have seen Nam with different eyes though. Not too much of a developing country anymore because there's so much potential for its future.

Back in the days before 1975[1], Vietnam was still at war with America. In one of those small rural villages lying to the north of Hue province, among millions of Vietnamese people who lost their families through war and sickness, hunger or nature calamities, a baby boy lost his mother through her labor not long after giving birth to him. There he grew up with an older sister together with his father and a stepmother.

Among the harsh exterior situations, they did not carry a family full of loving memories neither between two little kids from the previous wife, and the stepmother, my grandfather said. He recalled

---
1 The US - Vietnam War started from 1955 and ended in 1975.

since some time he turned four or five that he had to do many things, and started to carry his younger step-brother on his back to school everyday when he grew up a little more because no one was there to look after any of them.

I was born as the second post-war generation in my family, Tran Family, and for many times in my life I feel grateful to be raised afar from this tragic period. When I grew up, we did not talk much into details about the Vietnam War, both wars, and many more of them. We had had enough of "wars" in our family, and even in our heads.

When one got too used to something, it gradually became a part of one's lifestyle by default. There was a simple word we could use to describe our situation though, probably some might argue that anywhere but certain classes in the south of Vietnam, "poverty". There were many curious myths and horrible stories related to the constant famine and poverty during the consecutive wars and even after we gained Independence, especially in the rural area and countryside. As we had to face a massive shortage of food supplies, people had to be creative and learn to shape their diets in various ways. I remember my uncles told us how they prepared meals or got to adapt in such strict situations, they might mix rice with all kinds of tubers like sweet potatoes or cassava and that was still the best scenario for some days.

The most horrible one was during my grandfather's younger days, they had to look for this genus of crustaceans, "moina" or what we called *"con bo bo"* in Vietnamese, from the pond or rice field, for replacing the protein and enzyme source from the scarce resource of "conventional" food supplies. One of my uncles, uncle H., had to throw up when he listened to the story for the first time according to my grandfather. We all laughed at this tale, me and my cousin T., and later on, we admired him even more when we found out that he was eating rice with dead ants as our family had to save every single gram of rice at home. A "colony" of ants accidentally landing on our leftover rice on an afternoon could not turn his hunger into zero.

People could move from time to time to avoid war conflicts or potential dangers from hidden bomb traps or regional battles in real time, hence they constructed temporary huts with coconut leaves, bamboo and some sorts of fiber from local plans. Most of them worked as farmers for local plantation owners. My grandfather's hometown was famous for producing rice like the majority of the rural area in Vietnam, and especially aromatic and well spicy chillies.

Until one day he decided to leave their little house in the countryside of Hue province to the Imperial city, alone and discreetly. As I grew up listening to the same story plot line, I could picture these abruptly changed contexts quite well until even now. It sounds hilariously sad yet sarcastic that I ended up following that little boy's "footsteps" who was actually my grandfather and repeated this appealing idea when I was a teenager. I had never asked myself if my grandfather felt the same at that point, a little déjà-vu scenario run by the same bloodline with which he shares.

However, back in earlier childhood, I was not sure whether I would follow him even after listening to his life adventure tale endless times already. The story started to be exciting yet intrepid if not that crazy.

By his age, I enjoyed the privilege of being a kid which was to be careless and innocent. Even though I had certainly shared my fair part of being thoughtful and sensitive, I would have never planned to run away from our place. Maybe it was simply clear that I had been taken care of to a certain degree, left to my own devices so I could go discover the neighborhood, and then most of all I had lived a beautiful childhood – one not like my grandfather's until I could not anymore.

He left with apparently nothing but only one set of clothes and a well-worn-out pair of sandals. Did he walk or ask for a ride to the city? I do not remember that detail, as well he might have not told me about this transportation affair or probably I had never paid attention to this detail.

By the time he arrived in Hue city, it was already late afternoon. Yet the beauty of the Huong river had never failed anyone, especially someone who might see it for the first time like my grandfather. He was mesmerized by such peaceful calmness despite the actual complicated situations between North and South Vietnam that the impressive Truong Tien bridge had been reformed, and standing still after being bombed for several times[2].

He kept wandering around the center and had no idea of what to do next, so he stopped by a random local house, sat there, and met his one-of-a-lifetime "savior"– the son of the house's owners. In the mind of the seven-year-old boy who achieved such a potent will and enough courage to rebuild his life in such a chaotic period in the country, he did not expect to meet someone with a kindred spirit and gentle manner like this young man. In my pictured-story memory, this young man was a bit chubby, clearly enjoying his ice cream on a beautiful summer afternoon after a working day in imperial Hue city and having the best life his family could offer back then– a space to start his own business as a tailor.

The encounter happened when my grandfather incidentally peeked through the main steel gate, and saw this young boy having his ice cream on the porch. My grandfather was completely hungry and

---

[2] From 1899 and 1969, the bridge had a total of three times collapsed into the Huong River due to the war.

tired, he could not resist looking away from the fresh thirst-quenching ice cream that just happened to be in his desperate sight. Somehow this caught the young man's eyes and enthusiasm. He called my grandfather, brought him to the little grocery store nearby, and got him a new ice cream.

Quickly later he asked what my grandfather was doing at that late time especially because he was just a kid. For certain, the city which was still under the war had a restricted hour schedule to wander around at night. My grandfather told him "everything" without hesitation while finishing his first ice cream after a very long time being withheld from any children's treats back home.

The young man then nodded his head and responded in a brief sure voice, "stay with me and help me, I will teach you to be a tailor, a good fine one."

Of course, my grandfather stayed. He lived in Hue city until he turned eighteen years old. And that will be the story for later.

II.

Strange is also a feeling

I came to live in Da Nang city with my grandparents when I was two years old and grew up there. I had many good memories and also bitter ones facing up with the constant tension between them if not to say that I was torn by the endless family conflict.

My grandparents have eight children together. I am the first child of my father who is the oldest brother among my aunts and uncles. We, on our part, did not see each other that much since he left me there to my grandpas. Bringing me to a coastal city indeed was the best decision he had ever made for me.

My father did not get married to my mother who was an Hoa ethnic child. Her family, whose ancestors are Chinese, moved to Vietnam before the Vietnam - America war. We call the Chinese immigrant community, Hoa ethnicity or so-called Hoa people, considered one of the fifty-two ethnicities in Vietnam.

I remember my paternal grandmother kept telling me back then that I did not speak Vietnamese at all when I was first introduced to them in Da Nang. My maternal family spoke mainly in Chiuchow[3] or *"tieng Tieu"* in Vietnamese despite being from Guangdong[4], hence I got my little Cantonese to express my wishes to go to the restroom, eat or drink even after moving to Da Nang. Obviously, I had to learn to communicate in Vietnamese and get to "start" all over again at that point, and thorough my life.

The next thing drawing in my memory could be when I was about to learn to write hand letters and send them to my father who had been living in Saigon long before meeting, then breaking up with my mother. They had a relationship conflict that in all respects was unsolvable. From his perspective, growing up with my maternal family would not create a good decent upbringing as my mother did not play her part well.

Therefore, one day my father schemed an "escape" for me by informing my maternal family of a

---
3 Cantonese rendering.
4 Guangdong was formerly Canton, a coastal province in South East China, borders with Hongkong and Macau.

birthday party forgery on the night before and catching the earliest train the day later to Da Nang. He kept my whereabouts in secret until I was nine years old. That was the year we knew about my mother's passing-away news.

In my reminiscence of my grandfather from my younger days, he was often calm and silent in his manner and determinative in his action. He never went to Saigon with me. The one who brought me to see my maternal grandmother after all those years of my "missing" was actually my paternal grandmother. We waited until my summer vacation and traveled to Saigon to "pay condolence" to my maternal grandmother, "*ba ngoai*"[5].

It was such a strange idea submerging a part of my reality into the mysterious depth of human connection. The pain of loss did not enter me back then. How and why? Where did the pain go?

Perhaps I did not share as "sufficient" memories about her as I wished. Yet somehow it proved what my father's family perceived from the fact that she

---

5 Guangdong was formerly Canton, a coastal province in South East China, borders with Hong Kong and Macau.

partly abandoned me and went on with her own personal matters. The only dear time I could recall was when we shared a night's sleep together, my mother, my Little uncle who was actually spending more time with me than she did, and me.

He was older than me, about ten or eleven years old according to my father. There would be times when I woke up from a nap and cried for someone to be there with me while seeing no one. Little uncle would run to me and caress my hair, wipe my cheek, then pour all of his vintage vitro agate marbles on the floor so I could play with them. Sometimes he would carry me by his hip to where ba ngoai sold "Pho"[6], located on a random street spot in front of a huge mansion on Pho Duc Chinh Street, which is known as Ho Chi Minh Museum of Fine Arts nowadays.

I could recall the familiar aroma of Pho wandering around my little hammock where ba ngoai carefully knotted its ties to the iron gate bars by the long wall, right behind a typical humble carriage designed for street food vendors – the type that one could still see it until now, in order to watch me while working as hard as possible to nurture her family. Once in a

---
6 A popular Vietnamese soup dish consists of broth, rice noodle, herb and meat, claimed to be found first in Northern Vietnam culinary.

while from the clipped hammock veils, she would appear and gaze at me with attentive eyes then suddenly curse with a dear accent, something in Cantonese then in Vietnamese, "*cha may*", "your cursed father", and smiled gently at me. She was trying to put me to bed on a night street in Saigon, and on no account I will forget her face at that moment.

There was sort of an unexplainable chain of memories dwelling in my mind about when I lived in this house, and my father had to wonder in his utmost astonishment how I could remember all of these while having merely two years old. He even questioned my integrity and whether I went to meet someone and that "someone" would have told me all of these little details. Because they all carry out the fact – but not a made-up story in my desperate hours of longing for where my other half origin came from.

It was a full-moon night in Saigon, we laid still in the attic where they opened the only window and let the night zephyr stray in our little space. There was often a pack of wild cats wandering around the neighbor's rooftop, and calling each other out loud with a peculiar language. I was frightened and could not sleep, and tried to nestle to my mother. Gradually my Little uncle would suggest letting me sleep between them so I would feel safer, and indeed I did. In some bizarre ways, life twisted and turned and shaped itself deliberately, I never remember her face even through the unique memory about her. Somehow that might be the last night I spent time with her, anything that came later and before this night, became empty like a vacant house as if there were someone trying to erase all of the recorded memory from a mix-tape, leaving no music within this predestined empty space between us.

None of us has ever discussed this relationship I had got with my mother and her family. No one had ever prepared me for any of this. I was there, seeing my maternal grandmother for the first time after a long time. She was crying and looking at me at the same time, speaking with me something in Cantonese and later in Vietnamese with a scornful tone, "why did you not come to see me? It was your father's fault, all of this was his fault..." I could picture everything vividly in my mind just like that. My grandma sat beside me and held my left hand as tight as if she could squeeze some courage out of this awkward situation. She was nervous too, and I knew it even back then. It was the first time she encountered my mother's mother whose daughter had just died at the age of thirty-something. She had to carry me during those years when she got older after taking care of my aunts and uncles. Now she had to bring me to pay a visit to the living and the dead in that old house.

There was certainly something emotional about the situation, however, I could not feel anything but such constant turbulence in my gut. I felt strange. I kept asking myself why I was there and what I had to do to end this uncomfortable meeting. The visit was peak when my maternal grandmother asked me to hug her, and I, with all of my shyness, honesty, and my skinny body withdrew myself into even a smaller one and then answered, "no, I can not, I feel estranged to you." She cried even harder and I felt worse. I just knew that I hurt her even though it was not my fault, all of these intertwined affairs among adult people just happened to fail on me as a kid.

Once in a while I still wish I could have said something nicer or even explained better what I might feel at the moment than just a few honest words.

Luckily my grandmother helped me explain that I was always shy and especially to people whom I meet for the first time. Ba ngoai, even seemed taking it better after the brief interpretation, shook her head and kept murmuring, "yet I was there taking care of you when none of your parents was." Briefly they changed the conversation to my mother's death. Ba ngoai wept quietly and tried to suppress her emotional state by this stage of the meeting. She looked into the distance while recovering her memory of my mother's last days, she was doing just fine if not saying that she got better. She was in consecutive years of depression and did not work much so ba ngoai had to maintain selling street food as a main income of the whole family. At the moment we went to see ba ngoai, she was no longer selling pho as I remembered but changed to serve *"hu tieu"* instead[7].

---

7 A popular noodle dish either served as a soup or without broth in dry version, originally from Southern Vietnam.

My Little uncle had always been such a good boy, already set out to work and assisted her financially. He was living with another uncle of mine then as a dispute between him and another brother had happened not long after my mother's funeral. After all, they found my mother's death shockingly sudden, especially my Little uncle. Ba ngoai said to an invisible vacancy in front of her instead of looking at us, "the youngest brother of P. has, come what may, taken care of her and loved her dearly."

As they might have tried to avoid mentioning something, the conversation seemed to be going on in such a cryptic atmosphere where I collected a few common words like "normal", "nothing curious", and "pictures". Then it came to an end when I discovered that there was another person laying up "there" in the attic above us, listening to the conversation without uttering a word. It was my mother's older sister. As she knew that she could not ignore us anymore, she asked me if I wanted something to drink with her head hanging upside down toward where we sat. I said no madam, thanked her and gazed stiffly to the floor. Later on, we got two cans of Pepsi that my aunt insisted on bringing with us, and a bunch of my mother's newest pictures as souvenirs which someone took for her a week before her passing.

In those pictures, she always posed in the same manner – crossing her legs on one side and looking away from the camera without smiling. She seemed like a statue and showed no emotion on this half of her face. Her head tilted slightly toward the shoulder opposite to the camera, hence from where we captured the figure, I could not say whether I looked like her or not.

Ba ngoai cleared my doubt as if she could read my mind. Gently she commented that in fact, I looked more like my father, especially with my smile yet I got my mother's eyes, the sad almost sobbing ones.

After that meeting, we did not exchange a word related to it in any conversation. As if my grandmother, everybody and I had a quiet deal back then that since we stepped out of that house in District One in Saigon, anything had happened and whoever we met, remained there. Besides that abnormal meeting and the silent pact I got with everyone, I passed the left of the summer vacation full of fond memories with my cousin T., my grandmother, my aunts and uncles who live and work in Saigon, and my father. Yet I did not talk about what I heard and felt to anyone ever.

We went back to Da Nang one month later. As if this silent pact was a deal among adults, my grandfather did not ask me a word about the other part of the vacation. At the current point, I did not think that one day I might come back to that house in District One again, and on my own, and again.

It was early spring in Vietnam and also the "first" Tet which I had celebrated after missing four of them while living in Spain. Even though I tried to compensate for it by retaining the rituals of cooking a banquet and offering to who-know-god and decorating with flowers and fruits at my humble apartment in Madrid, it was nothing to compare with the authentic Lunar New Year. Yet I thought that if once I was back home celebrating the same thing we always do, those old days might be retrieved then and, it was not.

One's mind could play any genre of music without instruments and without a single band. It kept playing in oblivion, a soulful dimension of such magical geography – in every shape and at any time. In some given situations one must change for the better. The nostalgia was indeed tough even when I had already been back and walking such hidden music that my childhood had played, it did not sound the same anymore. I did not feel like I belonged anywhere. Somewhere in between I had found myself homeless. That little child seemingly got lost and left behind an emptiness in my memory.

At some points, I told myself to give up the illusion of walking such an old beaten path as if there was a ghost dangling at the back of my mind, the ghost of the bygone past, and this very same grey ghost kept whispering the same old things over and over again.

I came back to the area where my mother and her family used to live in District One Saigon. I followed the memory "tape" and was unsure of which alley there had to be. Neither I remembered the exact address which was printed on my mother's Death Certificate. Simply I kept walking along Pho Duc Chinh Street and turned to a random alley. The alley was narrow and looked better than what appeared in my memory hence I took it with ease. Somehow I had always felt a bit threatened and scared to know about my maternal side. A well-trained habit developed by a constant reminder from my paternal side of how cruel and ill-educated the "other" side might be since I grew up. Up till this point, I had to shake off all of these biased ideas and take my own chance to discover what might be "left". However, I had never hated my mother for what they said or not about her.

At the end of the alley, highlighting the whole atmosphere was a typical Hoa shrine yet as small as a motorbike garage, and as high exactly as the average height of an Asian figure. Notwithstanding the two-level altar was essentially well-decorated with red bulb lights, candles, and many offerings that this little shrine suddenly spoke of itself more than the living creatures around. The smoke from lighted-up incense was still hanging around the air, I could notice the tidiness from every detail of which such a shiny clean space the shrine presented. From there the left pillar which was carved with the Chinese blue and green dragon, sinking behind a heap of miscellaneous kinds of stuff arranged in different categories, an old and grumpy face started to attain my attention. At first glance, one would think this creature was squatting behind the low plastic table as she crouched forwards and leaned both of her elbows on the knees.

She was patiently looking at me for a while and waiting for me to speak first. She knew that I was not a casual visitor who got lost in this little alley. Right at the moment our eyes crossed for the first time as I had tried to ignore her stare for as long as I could, she lifted her head straight and gave me a bold look. She threw her patience away and asked strictly. "Muon gi?"[8] I was not scared at all yet interestingly acknowledged her manner as somewhat as familiar as the way my father described my mother's neighbors around this area.

I pointed at the bunch of goods she was selling on the table after noticing a few Vietnamese coffee filters[9] on the table as well, "you are selling coffee too?" She

---

8 Meaning "What do you want?" but in an extremely rude way as the local woman does not use a subject to address in the conversation. Hence the author wants to leave this part in the origin Vietnamese.
9 A special coffee brewing set of tools including a plate, a chamber and a filter press which is frequently made of stainless steel.

replied immediately, "of course," her face started to relax and I knew she tried to paint a content smile with a strange customer. "I would like a glass of *"ca phe sua"*[10] with less milk. May I sit here too?" She nodded, "sit, take one of those chairs." I sat down at a red plastic one, waiting for the making of street coffee, the kind with less condensed milk and adding ice or without as one's favor.

I stirred the small ice cubes in my glass and at that moment I almost gave up the idea of searching for my mother's old house as it had never been that important to me. Many times my father had mentioned the same thing that the old house was sold, there is only one older sister of my mother living there with her husband who is working as the Leader of that neighborhood residential group. He is a veteran now after serving several terms in the Vietnam-America War which took the final heat in Saigon. He lost one arm and was compensated with a shared huge house on a busy main street in the center. He sold the house altogether with other co-owners for money, bought and built a house right

---

10 Coffee with condensed milk.

where my mother's family used to live and moved in with his wife, who is my aunt. The old house was divided and shared for profit between brothers and sisters while some of them passed away from cancer or sudden death, there are only two members left. I wonder if I wanted to come to say hello to this aunt. I never had any contact with any of them as my father warned me to keep my distance from them since the last time I met the older uncle. That was the summer I went to Saigon alone for the first time.

The grumpy woman noticed that I was pondering yet she knew I was going to open up about whatever I had "schemed" to ask her like a witty tiger had been taking its time for the gazelle losing its patience and starting to run in fear toward such a vast and vague desert of information. "I don't know if you have any news about a woman named P., she passed away around twenty years ago. Her family lives or used to live here around this neighbourhood." While asking her with unclear resources, I pointed somewhere toward the southeast direction from where I sat. She seemed intrigued but still could not figure out whom I was talking about. I mentioned, "my grandmother used to sell Pho along Duc Chinh Street and..." She suddenly disrupted my terrible explanation and as if she had discovered a scarce well among the barren desert, her voice busted into such a strange high pitch voice. "Your mother was named E., not P.! And you are that little kid from her with the boy from Da Nang!" Blending among surprises and "coincidental" storylines I had collected, I remember that detail about my mother's dear nickname her family called her because of the way it was rendered in Cantonese. She also added that I do not look that much like my mother but the eyes. Perhaps she could come to the conclusion thanks for this detail.

Notwithstanding, I had been even more excited about the fact that the alley I chose was the exact one leading to my mother's old house when I noticed the number of the alley nailed on the house facade cross to our location. It was the same numbers I had always looked at but did not bother to remember every time I had to refill some kind of paperwork.

There was an abrupt silence afterward that made me notice her facial expressions just simply changed, darker and even more grumpy than the first time I saw her. She could be a good storyteller yet her Vietnamese was chopped up sporadically even

though with an assertive tone. At this same moment, our eyes crossed one more time and I could never figure out what she was going to tell me next. Her eyes darkened under the shadow of an old patio umbrella, she showed me her arm and gestured meaningfully with an imaginative syringe in her hand on the other side under my astonishment while having to figure out what she tried to hint at. "Your mother...," she slowly nodded her head, "*played* too much of this." She tilted her head towards her arm while drawing a repugnant smile that made me want to run away immediately from that terrible moment.
So it had been a lie all of this time about my mother and I had to go figure it out on a random day from a random creepy street vendor who accidentally knew everything about my mother's family. She could not shut up about that, "you can not find anyone here but a sister of your mother. You want to see them?" At this second she changed her eyesight for the first time and gestured toward someone behind me. I tried not to show up my terror while slightly turning my back and looking over my shoulder. A man with a friendly smile had been sitting there and listening to us for some time I barely knew. When he knew that

he could not play silent anymore, he started to repeat what the vendor said, "yes we could help you call them. The sister is probably there."

I realized that I started to tremble. My blood ran out my head like a speed train, leaving an empty place in my confused brain trying to think about possible refusal among these strangers yet who happened to know my mother better than me. I mumbled and tried to give a bright smile, "hm I don't think it's necessary. I might disturb her," and finished the drink. The vendor took an effort and raised her voice under my dreaded eyes because she almost shouted at me. "Why is it bothering her? It is a part of your family!"

Until this point, my legs wanted to move so hard but my head kept it cool and said the truth, "no, I do not want to see any of them." She started to laugh out loud in a cinematic way and speak jokingly in a sarcastic tone, "so now she does not want to see her family."

I walked away after uttering a brief goodbye to both of them without looking back. I was so frightened that I thought if I had turned my head back, the man would keep me there while the woman was running to my relative's house to announce my presence and they would never let me go. It all felt so strange that I swore to myself, I probably would never set foot again in that alley.

A part of you died as you knew that a few important people in your life passed away without you being there. What on Earth was important to come back if they were no longer there, my grandmother, my mother and my little uncle?
My father was right. At first, he always sounded illogical and rational at the same time but as it turned out, he had his reason to warn me about this neighborhood.

III.

Between the city of bridges
and
the city where Saigon river flows

Da Nang has nine (or ten?) bridges in total. We could have mentioned the Golden Hand one in Bana Hill, yet personally, I do not think it should be counted as the Han river's upstream does not start from the hill either run across it. Then there are actually three other bridges constructed on the Cam Le river.

I happened to grow up when Da Nang was in its fierce developing period between 1998 and 2008. Due to those ten years and probably has it advanced further, many things and places have both disappeared and grown along the river banks, and kept expanding.

In the memoir extracted from one of the hand-letter collection sending to his lover[11], the composer Trinh Cong Son recalled this city was much more boring than Hue imperial city around the America - Vietnam war period. Barriers spread along the riverside,

---

[11] As known, "Love Letter to A Person" by the composer Trinh Cong Son.

curfews had to be imprinted in one's mind, postal mail got lost or delayed for months, and more than all, it was difficult for people to travel from place to place. Then everything changed, even not quite swiftly.

After making his debut as a young tailor in Hue city, my grandfather went back to his hometown for the first time when he was eighteen years old and met my grandmother at the same time. His older sister could not stop crying as she had done so for the past eleven years when they encountered him "in the flesh".

They were looking for him everywhere around the village, the coast and the forests close by, any lake, pond, and river, and even in every single well surrounding the neighborhood. Without further hope and attempt, they came to the worst conclusion that he might have gotten lost and passed away somewhere in the wild. He told me that he could see his picture with a child version of himself on the altar back in the same house.

He told me nearly nothing about his personal and intimate moments in life except this part where he met my grandmother, went to talk with her, wrote her letters and song lyrics then asked her to be his wife. Things were simpler back then and somehow were more romantic. My grandmother was eighteen years old for a few days when she got married. My grandparents moved to Da Nang city quickly after a humble wedding in the same summer.

I had not mentioned that my grandmother is illiterate. She did not have many chances to go to class, and even when she had got it once, she was too tired to study while taking care of her younger brother and sister. She might have always made up many reasons for this fact about her. The war was difficult for everyone, she had to take responsibility as the older sister together with an older brother. Then she got married too early and got carried away by children, family, and living earnings. This fact might affect her own life significantly but it never makes me think anything less about my grandmother.

Until now every single corner of the old house has still imprinted vividly in my memory, and my dreams. Even in those dreams, they surged to my subconsciousness as a profound message, a haunted moment or simply a heavily emotional trace back to the past.

Most of my childhood and years of younger adolescence happened in this old house. It was a space labyrinth first of all to my own eyes at first then quickly I "grew" larger than the house itself consciously – it became a corner of buried emotions, existential crises, and broken dreams. Somehow I felt like I had left all of these "secrets" behind once we had to tear it down in half and sell the other one to a far relative. My life began again and drastically changed afterward. During the up-and-down moments in our family, I attempted to run away from it at any cost.

The house in which we shared had a typical old-style living room where we could build and decorate the altar a few meters in front of the main door and beside a small bedroom, a bathroom with a "curious" well which was the center of every cleaning relative activities – a laundry room, dishwashing room then we would wash our face or take showers by turns, then a kitchen, an adjacent space between the living room where it would lead to the kitchen then a toilet – this weird structure was seen as a good place to put a bed or two so all of us except my grandfather, would sleep here together, in a two-person bed or on the floor. Yet the house did not stop there. Connecting to the toilet was a narrow open-air alley running along the right side of the house which ended in the bathroom. From this little breezy alley, my grandfather's bedroom window would open on sunny days and close tight in the rainy season. We could only hang our clothes on dry days which started from the beginning of March until late September or the beginning of October. Of course, there would be sudden summer rain occasions when we had to hurriedly run and collect our laundry so as to hang them back again because they were getting the fresh rain shower, and the sun was done with playing hide-and-seek.

The concrete ground level of the alley was descending toward the bathroom which formed a unique concrete platform working as the only stair. Hence we would have to be careful every time we walked up and down through it. From this concrete stair, I would sit down to enjoy an ice cream in a breezy afternoon, spend time reading comics or rehearsing homeworks. On full-moon nights, I would follow such silvery magical moonlight to the alley that was shined up entirely, and imagine I could talk to someone "up there" on the Moon from this little place on Earth. I could stand there for a while and keep my eyes gazing upon the dreamy velvety night sky.

For many times when I felt sad and abandoned, the alley or the dusty small space behind the altar would be where I searched for an emotional refuge. It is easier to cry when nobody is around. Nobody could bother one's feelings and interfere with the reason why one might feel such melancholy since ever one was a child. Because one was scared to be unable to understand one's own feelings, and it would be a crime to cry without a single reason in aldults's logical mind.

The central region of Vietnam is prone to frequent natural disasters, particularly flooding and typhoons, which occur almost every rainy season and cause significant damage to the coastal communities. When a tropical storm hits, the heavy rain can persist for days, posing infrastructure damages and even life-threatening situations. Essential supplies could become scarce, and power outages are inevitable. Schools and other activities would be suspended, especially fishing activities, both near and far from the shore must come to a halt.

I vividly recall the scenes of us desperately bailing water out of our house while trying to salvage our belongings by placing them on the highest, driest spots available. Meanwhile, my grandmother's bed suffered from the relentless drizzle leaking through the roof, dampening the hallway and kitchen.

During the peak of the storm, we had to don raincoats even inside our own home and prepare a ready-to-go handbag. It was a precautionary measure in case of an unexpected evacuation, or simply to protect ourselves from the rain pouring in through damaged or blown-away rooftops anytime.

There followed the other end of the bathroom, which would be the front porch, however, this part was built quite not open as the alley. In contrast, one could not enter the porch deliberately as it was covered by a tall wall up to the roof and a heavy large iron gate.

We were living under an epoch where we had always been alert not only about our security, yet also our own privacy. We did not ever wish anyone to peek into our daily activities or steal our bicycles while taking a nap. Even nowadays, Vietnamese families would feel "safer" living among immensely high walls with securely well-designed main gates, front doors, and windows. The thicker the wall is, the better it will be.

Notwithstanding I had always enjoyed playing right by the porch or at the side door of the house leading to the alley. As a child I had already established a clear intention of staying outdoors and enjoying that bit of open air. Those were the only spots where I could look at the blue and sometimes cloudy fragments of the sky, and take a cheerful sunbathe despite what my family might say about how my skin would turn brown, the beauty social norm of being a "brown skin" person.

I remember there was a period where I only took naps right by a "mega" window on the high wall by the porch because this was the unique one without folding doors like others, instead, simply covered by a changeable veil, leaving a third of it exposed. I would wake up under the frying afternoon sun or with eyes gazing at the half-blue half-cloudy window.

As well for some time, I schemed to let my neighbors borrow my comics and in return, I would collect brand-new rubber bands as a hobby. If the borrowers could not fulfill the condition, they had to pay me some pennies instead. Funnily it turned out that I earned much more money than rubber bands. In order to let people know about my comics collection and introduce my "business", I had to write an announcement on a piece of carton and put it on top of the columns of comics which I had arranged into different categories. By leaning on the wall, the carton table clearly spoke for me "RENTING OUT COMICS", and my job was to sit there with a comic in my hand and wait for my potential customers. My grandfather would peek through the only window connecting the living room as well his working space and the porch, and ask me what else I was planning this time. I explained and quickly he shook his head, "who could possibly read what you write on the carton? It is too little, no one can see anything." Then he suggested hanging it on the main gate instead.

I was extremely excited to listen to his advice and shared with him my little contentment by showing the quickly-earned pennies on the same day. One thing about this gesture that spoke meaningfully about us was that we were on the same page at least for some time.

I grew up with all sorts of rules in the house. From what time I had to be home at night to how I must respectively address elders and adults, from how to wash the dishes to at what tone one could speak without making too much noise. Especially when it came to following orders and demands from the "grow-ups", I had to avoid talking back, and keep silent. Yet I tended to break this part up if there were any "incorrect" claims addressing my behaviors and manners which had seemed relatively one-sided. I had always been the type of person who could hardly ever stand for unfair judgments toward both myself and other people. I would try to protect myself, my cousins, a neighbor or even a classmate with whom I barely had a good relationship. This kind of heroic character sometimes brought me troubles and led to worse situations, in which I turned out to be a villain in adults' eyes instead. My family kept calling me the little rebel and all kinds of terrible things, stating that my future could be ruined if I continued to be such a "doggery". Until my family recognized my class and school prize collections at every school year-end event, then graduated from secondary school excellently, and proved that there was nothing to do with my behaviors as they had worried. These childhood names remained a triumphant call to my true self then.

However, the rapture of studying prizes did not draw me in that long because quickly I realized that, life in its own sense, should mean much more than chasing someone else's approval.

Later on in my life, I kept coming back to Da Nang and every old corner as much as possible. Altogether with Hoi An ancient town, they both had witnessed some of my most beautiful moments and yet saddest in life.

I traveled with my father by train to Da Nang in 1996 according to all the events and timelines in which I had connected through stories and my profile papers. At that moment, my grandparents were still around their fifties, robust and content at least about what they had. Even though they had experienced a year-long famine after the General Offensive and Uprising[12] in the spring of Mau Than 1968, which the American army would call "Offensive Tet"[13], and a war that lasted until 1975, they still remained together.

There were good memories and bad memories in this old house as I always remember. Just like that, I moved into it where I would discuss with my youngest aunt, aunt Lo. who was seven years older than me, to pick which toy we wanted, and which gift we might get from my grandmother as well her mother. We had shared quite a queer period when we grew up, as we had a little age distance but must see each other in appropriate roles. She is my aunt and I am, as always, her little niece.

---

12 Viet Cong or Liberation Army of South Vietnam or the National Liberation Front of South Vietnam, and North Vietnamese People's Army of Vietnam, started the campaign right before New Year Eve's 1968.
13 Tet is Lunar New Year Eve, following lunar calendar and the most important holiday celebrated in Vietnam.

It was as well when I got a bit indulged by another older aunt, aunt L. who would buy many toys and clothes for me, gave me some pocket money to spend for breakfast and snack time, or even bring me with her while hanging out with her girlfriends, and boyfriends with whom she might change once every while. She has been always my favorite one in the family. I cried like hell with myself at night when she got married and had to live at her husband's house as a Vietnamese traditional custom in marriage in the past, probably it still lasts somewhere until nowadays.

I have another aunt, aunt H. who is the oldest sister of the three but is still younger than my father. She used to support me in finance for a few years when my father could not take care of me economically. Indeed he was never significantly present for any important events in my life except for some times, he would help me buy what I needed for studying.

The train we took together from Saigon to Da Nang when I turned two years old was probably the first and the last trip we shared together.

From there I learned to speak Vietnamese and completely forgot my poor Cantonese. Then I wrote my first letter to my father under the instruction of aunt L. when I was six or seven years old. She taught me a lot of things too, and when she scolded me for my mistakes, I recalled her sad face then holding me in her arms, she would bring me to buy some snacks as a way of spiritual comfort.

After running away from my grandparents' house in 2010, I moved in with her and her husband's rental places. During this period of six months, we moved and changed our living spaces five times. Despite the economic difficulty, her cook as always was my second spiritual comfort after reading, until it could not anymore.

I met my childhood friend D. here and shared my imagination with her for a very long time that I could have not imagined my life any different without her. We met in a local kindergarten when we were four years old. Within a year later I could read and write perfectly as I told you that I practiced writing letters to my father thanks to my aunt. Nevertheless, I learned to read quite fast due to the fact that I had a huge passion for anime and manga, especially Doraemon. I would see him, and all together with D.

as my most dear friends in the "Universe" even up till now. With D. we shared many good memories together, then a few sad ones happened when we turned into adolescents and studied in different high schools.

I do not recall what I might tell her about my family, my "little situation" back then. The highlight of our shared childhood was that we lived and spent time together with our utmost innocence. We often walked by the beach close to home at night and talked nonstop about a certain anime character, which usually would be D. because she has an enormous collection of Japanese comics since back then already, our last-night-dreams as yes, we are probably the few people who remember our dreams to details when we wake up, my lonely feelings, for some time, and her complexed "affair" with literature (she was an excellent student at this subject for many years). I have felt lucky to meet and befriend her. Our connection has a bright light shedding over my life through many periods except the one I ran away.

The most fun memory was when we poured our effort into "creating" our own comics when we were nine years old. Even though I am not sure who would come first with the idea, we were pretty much on the same page about everything. We would decide on the storyline and the characters which we borrowed and were inspired by Doraemon and Pikachu's main characters. Sometimes D. sketched or wrote the conversations, other times I did. We always made sure we shared every work together. I even invented a corner at the back of the comic "book" so we could communicate with our "readers". We would have the whole project working like this, I would bring each episode to a nearby photocopy shop, and ask to print a three-page story – the kind of page size we took from our school notebook back then, in five copies which were costing us one thousand Vietnam dong at the moment. Then we sold each copy for one thousand dongs and would earn four thousand dongs as "profit". D. sold really well in her primary school class as it was the excellent one filled with good finance families. For my part, I tried to compensate with ideas, work, and bring them to copy. We kept writing and copying until we earned twenty thousand dongs in profit in total. Her mother figured this out and asked us to stop because we needed to focus on studying, we had to graduate from primary school soon.

I do not remember what else we did later on after splitting the profit. In my own case, I probably kept buying Doraemon and Detective Conan, collecting many episodes then left them for rent again as my personal project. This time I earned two thousand dongs of profit. Then I kept being busier with studying after figuring out that I was dragging behind in my class. However, during the last two years of primary school, I kept being ranked within the top three. Then consecutively in four years of secondary school, I got the first rank in class and second prize in Biology in a city competition. My studying path turned in many ways, yet I know I am always the one who decided it my way.

There was a summer I recalled, I might have hurt D.'s feeling a great deal by lying to her that I was about to move and live in Saigon "forever". Meanwhile, it was just a short summer trip to Saigon and I would not be able to see her for some time. I reckon it was the summer of 2003, we were in the most beautiful period of our friendship while exchanging sort of

"Friendship Journals" with colorful glittering pens and typical anime or illustrative stickers. We would take turns to fill them with our best calligraphy of amazing sayings, poems and quotes about how valuable true friends, and real friendship might be in our life. I do not understand why I had to make up this kind of break-up situation, and leave a little scar on someone's heart, including myself like that.

It was my first time back in Saigon after living in Da Nang for many years. Moreover, it happened to be the first time I was brought to visit ba ngoai and offer incense to my mother's altar. Honestly, I did not know what was supposed to occur within the following years when I felt like the trip could change my spirit in some way. I had always pictured Saigon as the cooler city to live in, due to the fact that all of my aunts and uncles came there to look for better jobs and build their careers. Perhaps I got the idea to sun away and establish my own life from such a model through time subconsciously.

There was a deep secret wish that I tried to negate when it entered my mind. Because of my so-called childlike pride, my timidity, and my narcissistic loneliness, I wished maybe, maybe my father would ask me to stay and live with his family in Saigon back then.

I imagined that once every while I would call D. from there, tell her about how life might be in the big city, promise her to come back and spend summertime together. But nobody talked about that, the wish quickly became a lie in order to sustain the fantasy of a kid – being able to stay closer to her father. Later on, I realized that I negated the wish as I did not want to feel abandoned by my father which would hurt me even much more.

I can not make an excuse for the fact that I lied to D. because of my vulnerability. I should have shared this deep secret wish with her instead, as I had once told her about my adolescent sorrow that my father had indeed abandoned me. D. was the only person to whom I recognized this fact.

We planned to bring our best photos as souvenirs to each other on the last rendezvous. After exchanging the last quotes in the Friendship Journal, I got to keep the second one of the two volumes collection, and then we said goodbye. We cried and promised not to forget each other. D. gave me a piece of paper with phone numbers, her father and mother's name written on it, "call me some time please," she said.

In the same summer, not long before the new school year began again, D.'s mother caught me at the neighborhood alley by contingency, strolling through street food kiosks and hesitatingly picking an item for breakfast. She was clearly surprised by my presence at the moment, and asked me how on Earth I was still around. I responded that there were a few "technical errors" and that I had to come back to live here with my grandparents.

She did not suspect about my plan or perchance she did have a doubt about my ambiguous explanation. However, she reminded me to visit D. whenever I could, she would be happy to see me. Yet it did not happen as I had thought. I saw D. hanging out with her cousins and sister quite well, without me, when I came to see her by surprise.

My presence had been a surplus in someone's life, quickly the cursed thought ran through my head. By nine years old, I felt like nothing had ever mattered again and on the other hand, I wished I would hang out with D. "forever".

After the trip, there were two things I was sure of the air was so pregnant with changes, and I officially lost my mother.

Growing up a little more I had many dreams, one of those was to leave this city on my own, and just like that I did.

IV.

What happened in Saigon? - Part One

I never know what was the deal between my father, my grandparents, and my aunts. They took care of me in turns and sometimes when difficulty came, I could feel such abandonment in their words and actions, yet even never that brutal like throwing me out of the house or pushing me into a hard work situation, I did see it and feel it. Most of all, especially from my father.
However, I neither wanted to believe in my own thoughts as my mental health was not steady and stable during when the conflict happened.
In my life, my father had hurt me several times in a great deal, and I reckon that I am not the only one he may have ever hurt. He had kept following the same trail for some time in his younger years until even now. People said he was getting better at shaping his own character, indeed I could see his positive effort and manner in recent years despite the relentless verbal violence.

On a summer morning in Saigon, during the time I "escaped", and got to concede that the plan was going wrong if I kept wandering without a job. My father convinced me to stay at uncle H.'s place temporarily because he failed to persuade my stepmother in real time to let me come over to their place.

We thought that was just fine as I did not feel comfortable sharing the space with them ever. In fact, they got divorced around six years later as it turned out that they had been living separately in different places for a while.

I still remember he was so nice and calm just the day before as we went to a bubble milk tea shop together, he even vouched for me as his patron when I asked for the part-time job.

According to the narrative from one of my uncle's workers, he would abruptly run into our bedroom, looking for where I slept as well as my luggage, dug all of my belongings out then tore apart my only English dictionary, my books, my diary, and tossed around my clothes. He pointed at me and kept repeating, he would not ever believe even one word I said. "Tell me", he continued repeating, "what do you come to Saigon for?" I insisted on telling him that he had done a very messy and nonsense thing, also with all my calmness and honesty I said I came to look for work while no one could take care of me at the moment.

He suddenly slapped one of my cheeks. A real hit that I could see nothing but darkness in my eye for an instant, and a whole dark sky in my mind. Immediately I just responded, "so you think I would be scared by being hit like this? You won't solve any problem with violence ever. Here my other cheek, just slap it too."

When he was about to do it, my uncle ran towards the quarrel and tried to separate us. He shouted at me for not behaving well and then told me to stay somewhere else. He also said to my father that he should have not made a scene in his own house like that. Uncle H. was also the one who let me stay in his same house five years later. His wife wanted to recruit me as she was looking for someone who could assist her in managing a souvenir store in Ben Thanh market. I worked there for exactly one year and one month after quitting Da Nang University.

Each time that event crossed my mind, I found my father shrinking in my memory – his once thunderous presence, his contorted face in such a simmering anger, and following so my own resentment and anger towards him gradually diminished day by day.

My father had a little business in tailoring back then in Da Nang when he was around nineteen and early twenty years old. Indeed he ran it well, earned good money, saved it then started to think further than his own town. I remember he told me about the first time he came to Saigon with the savings and a bicycle he bought himself in Da Nang. All were carried by bus for one day and one night. After the long hard trip there he was the only one left behind. Someone with their greedy atrocity or blaming it on cursed cruel life, stole my father's money and the bicycle while he was sleeping.

Everybody in my family said he was a nice guy if not saying very nice and decent one back home. Then off he changed. Even in my early day's memories of living in Da Nang, I still remember his frequent letters and calls to me as his only child. I would write my father season greetings cards and life-checking letters once in a while, and in return, I would receive a post card or letter from him.

There was a period, aunt L. and I would walk or ride her bicycle to a local post office and call my father from one of the three glass boxes. I waited patiently and uncomfortably as I was often not feeling familiar talking directly with my father. The constant distance could erode a connection in such an abstract bizarre way. Sometimes my grandfather would take a bicycle ride with me in the back seat to the office, discuss business plans with my father, then let me talk with him. I did not talk much though as one could imagine. I had always been a shy kid and grew up to be an introverted girl. I often thought to myself that I was the least favorable character in my big family as I seldom showed physical affection or "lovely" manners to anyone. Unlike my cousin T. who had always been able to show her affection to our grandparents like giving them hugs or kisses, and making them laugh by saying innocent jokes and "adult-like" statements, I was sort of a calm and "stoic" person. As if there were an invisible door between my inner world and the outside world, I kept distance from everything and everyone else except D. and my diary.

I discovered writing journals through an unforgettable event. When aunt Lo. went back to Da Nang after working with uncle H. in Saigon, she had a difficult time navigating around the "new" environment, dealing with my grandparents' affair, and what was to do next. She wrote all of these inner struggles and thoughts in her diary.

There was one time I tried to read what she was actually writing out of curiosity and learnt the basic outline, her writing style, her way of expressing emotions, and eventually the journal content as I did not know what I could write at the beginning of the practice.

Certainly until some point aunt Lo. caught me out "duplicating" her journal habit and especially her nostalgic emotion about life in Saigon.

She gave me a long lecture about how embarrassing it was to copy someone else's writing, moreover one should not reproduce other people's feelings as such. Since that time I kept going on writing as I knew "practice makes perfect". By and large, I tried my best to be creative in writing as well then.

Gradually I found it easier to put down my thoughts by simply talking with an invisible "friend" on endless blank pages. Through and through I knew that I was no longer doing it out of curiosity, journaling is indeed a friend to one's mind.

I started to write poems and short stories around eight years old. It would be about any silly things like an ode to watermelons, a lost white rabbit toy's journey, then meticulous proses in describing flamboyant trees or Indian almond trees, and memories weaved in with personal feelings. I tended to write creatively with a "free" mind, as we had always had to follow certain academic rules and outline in essay comments exercises. Even though I knew I would receive a lower mark than typical "outline" fellows, I was often excited to challenge myself by doing something dynamic and different.

Then home telephones were established in Da Nang, we would exchange our neighbor's phone numbers and keep each other in reach like that. I remember a random member of the neighbor's family would come to call us every time my father tried to reach out and share some news, we paid them a few dongs every half an hour which was usually the same latent plan.

During that peaceful period, my father would frequently visit us in Da Nang. While I have limited recollection of our activities together, they typically involved visiting my grandfather T.'s younger stepbrother or going on brief shopping excursions.
I recalled one time we went to see a dear friend of my father who lived in a decent leaf hut. He borrowed the Honda cup from grandfather T. and drove us a long way to her house. This woman just got divorced and was living with her little daughter about the same age as mine. I was eight as I could estimate and still remember that he kept repeating to me this woman was really poor, she got divorced from her husband and they were really close friends. I felt bad for the little girl so I tried to be friendly with her daughter as the two adults disappeared for a while after telling us to spend time together. Neither daughter nor I noticed their absence until they came

back. We left briefly later and never I heard about her nor come to see them again.

One summer he brought us all, aunt Lo., two cousins of mine T. and B., and me to the city water park. There at that point, I started to feel the emotional conflict I had got for my father.
I felt a sense of unease being in his presence, as if an intangible barrier separated us, and I knew that crossing that line meant embracing the roles of father and daughter. Like two independent nations, we established each other's "government" state in our own way yet we maintained a significant "foreign" affair. To me, he had always been such a foreigner to my world that even though he tried to obtain such a righteous "passport" to access my world, he seemed sadly an outsider, and he was. There was a period, he would ring the phone and let me speak with him then gradually he refused to call me. The last Christmas card he wrote me was when I turned nine years old. He kept silent afterward.
Those were cherished moments from the past, filled with sweetness, but little did I know they marked the beginning of a somber chapter that lay ahead.

When I turned eight, I got the news he was about to get married to a well-educated woman whose father was a lawyer. I saw this old man exactly two times in my life until I got the news that he just passed away this January. I still can picture his look at me when I was a kid then when I grew up and saw him again which I did not think that would be for the last time – a stoic one with a brush of calm eyesight and preserved gesture. I would say hello and he would just nod his head without saying anything else. However there was only one time he did talk a lot and that was when he flew to see my grandfather, stayed one night with us, and marched away the next morning.

This old man who happened to be my father's father-in-law was full of passion for complaining many things about my father's behavior at this stage. As if it had come to a certain massive point of sustaining my father's terrible temper, he must catch a flight in order to tell what he had to share with my grandfather. I did not understand a single matter in this adult's affair. I sat there and listened, and my grandfather did not say a word either. Finally, he said one simple thing that just shut this man off. "I am sorry but it is late, so I would like to ask your consent that I need to go to bed." Then they both went to bed after saying goodnight to each other.

I could feel the awkward atmosphere hanging in such silence, the robotic posture from both fathers, and the quiet anger from my grandfather's eyes. Later on, I discovered that he got angry not only at my father but also at this old man. Yet he did not scold my father or even raise his voice while talking with him on the phone. I knew back then he and my father exchanged essential respect for each other.

This happened when I was in my second year of secondary school.

I did never care about my father's affairs and private life as I hardly ever do. Until the ex-stepmother called me and complained about my father when I was seventeen years old and about to turn eighteen. This same year happened to witness many other important marks in my life.

She had almost never called me before and caught this time just to share with me how awful and violent my father could be. She mentioned the fact that he was trying to hurt himself on the same day and asked me to give him some comforting words. I was probably the only one to whom he might listen. She almost begged me to do this for the sake of my two step-brothers.

How was I supposed to feel about all of this? I did not know until even now. At that moment I felt like my father and I had just played a game that hurt each other and the people around us. This was, for the first time, I could realize what an improvised and childlike person we were... I was deeply unsettled, filled with concern, and continually carrying emotional traumatization. Time after time I could not breathe well and had chronic migraines. The only ways I sought to find solace and escape from reality, both physically and spiritually, were through the realms of books, writing, and running.

Despite the negative periods in our relationship, I had many beautiful moments with my father. I can not tell exactly how I did feel in those times between the two periods, nevertheless I am still an independent one who tries to thrive in my solitude.

In my longing reminiscence, when my father went back to his hometown for taking part in my youngest aunt Lo.'s wedding, one late afternoon he caught me writing on the front porch. As we had not maintained a close connection and on the other hand, I was already an unbalanced hormone teenager, things seemed even more awkward when it came to communicating.

Under the soft dim light penetrating weakly through the window, I was focusing on my journal and did not realize he was standing on the other end of the porch, lighting a cigarette. He blew into the air a few puffs before asking me what I was actually doing. I could be brusque if I felt like being disturbed by that age. Therefore I gave him an impatient answer, "I am writing my journal," to which I emphasized the possessive pronoun. Yet he continued. "Can I read it?"

As I wished to be left alone, I said no he could not, and that is why it was called a "journal". When he was about to finish the cigarette, before marching off, gently he told me, "you should start to write something that everybody could read, writing should be shared." That was one of the rare times in my life where he actually made me feel moving and proud of him because he did say something beautiful at least.

Did I really see him in me? Or what exactly had he done that I had to bear all of those dark marks with me even until now?

He never told me.

V.

This time I could tell you
about that escapism

Once upon a time, there was a little girl. She was always mesmerized every time she saw those high gleaming buildings in downtown Saigon. Especially at night when those billboards were lit up and luxury hotel windows just brightened the night sky and then every single lamppost was turned on endlessly. She could feel something dynamite about the nightlife in the city.

And so every time her father drove her to the riverbank, they would come across those hotel windows. She remembered that she insisted to her father, "papa, can you buy me those beautiful houses?" He did not laugh nor responded in a serious way, simply he just said, "you have to grow up and buy them yourself."

Then off he drove them both to this bank of Saigon river on an old bicycle, he would light up cigarette after cigarette and let her play with wildflowers on the pit dark tinted with such golden city light grass field. She still remembered the melody from an old song, "Dau chan dia dang"[14] written by *Trinh Cong Son* and performed by *Khanh Ly* singer, played on the radio by a street vendor who was also the one that sold those single cigarettes to her father. From the vivid canvas of her cinematic memory, she could effortlessly imprint a snapshot that flawlessly encapsulates the scene – the quiet atmosphere along the river bank, the scarce glimmers of light emanating from the distant side of the city across the flowing river, and the wisps of burnt cigarette smoke gracefully dancing before her eyes...

"Hey!" Suddenly he would call her, breaking the stillness of the moment. "Do not linger too close to the edge of the river," he would caution. With a swift and protective motion, he would reach out and rescue her from the precariousness of a potential fall, pulling her back into the safety of his embrace.

My mother and father, each of them had their own "century" melancholy, and from there they found each other, from there I was born. I wonder how a

---

14   The song name could be translated in a poetic way as the nostalgic traces left in heaven.

little child about two years old could remember such a conversation and those picture-like memories, even those haunting melodies of the old song could keep playing in one's mind through a single "tap" into reality. As if I were someone else who kept recording these vivid scenes without realizing that I would have to carry all of those fractional yet crystal-clear events throughout my life.

Later on, there was one time my father told me that he had to carry me by one hand, and on the other hand, he would drive his old bicycle to the central train station in Saigon. The night I recall may have been the last night I was there with him. He said he had to escape from Hoa people's street where it would never bring me any good if I grew up there. "Your mother was really cruel and lacked responsibility to you. Whenever I was back from work, I never saw her with you. She would let you crawl around alone and even get a burn from the neighbor's fire."

A part of the Vietnamese and Chinese tradition as it continues until now is to burn beautiful printed paper as a kind of offering and worship to their ancestors, or some invisible important Gods around their houses and from the land where they live. On one of those days, I happened to be nearby and got a burn on the lower part of my left calf.

The escapism passed down from my grandfather to my parents and then to me, I may say. We would seek a way to escape from whatever kind of reality we have to deal with. In my grandfather and father's case, they would run away from where they were born and lived. In another case, my father would look for tremendous "help" from alcohol, and I would try many ways until I figured out one, be it keeping on running away or simply staying alone.

There were those such fine afternoons before I turned ten, my grandfather had some free time from work and I did not have to go to school. After nap time, I would spend unbothered time and time just listening to his story.
My grandfather never liked his father and stepmother, I could sense the sheer anger and pain through the stories he kept repeating on telling me. He was very little when his father got married again.

He and his older sister would do a lot of the housework every day, if not they would be punished by being left hungry, scolded or simply not allowed to go to school. He told me that the stepmother would invent some naughty stories and tell them to his father when he was back from working at the rice field. My grandfather would end up being yelled at and locked inside the pigsty.

About this fact, as I remember one time his sister went to visit us, she would insist to forget it when she was about to cry but quickly swept her cheeks, and said "oh why you keep telling old stories, it is already in the past. We have to cheer up and live our life at this age."

She always left him a little money every time she visited us and a pocket one for me too. I realize that she was doing well in her life and now she has lived longer than my grandfather. Somehow she is right about the past, isn't she?

My grandfather tried to escape many times in his life. Not long after getting married to my grandmother, he was sent to join the local Viet Cong as an obligatory command to every young healthy man back then. They were still staying in a rural region in Hue at the moment a military enlistment letter was already sent home.

My grandfather disliked the war and so he tried to run and hide away from the draft notice.[15] Unfortunately, he got caught by a Viet Minh group, they had doubts that he was playing two faces and got him in jail for a while. Until the fourth day in prison, on the way moving to another post, he encountered an old friend who happened to work and got ranked Sublieutenant in the Viet Minh Front. This sublieutenant quickly recognized my grandfather and called for his release. He used his words to prove that my grandfather would never be a spy to "another side"[16], and he could use his ranking to vouch for my grandfather. They released him later.

The sublieutenant wrote him a letter and advised him to bring this to the region border so they could move to Da Nang safely in case they got in trouble again. Every time my grandfather told us about this breathtaking life and death moment again, my

---
15 Meaning like military enlistment call.
16 Implicating Ngo Dinh Diem Government.

grandmother would smirk as likely confirmed the fact, and leave the same comment, "even if he had got crushed by a pestle, he would have never died."

After that event, my grandparents left Hue to Da Nang for good. The political situation in Da Nang was more at "ease" at that moment, at least to the local area where they moved. He would keep working as a tailor and raise one or two pigs as a side business, yet he earned mostly from trading sewing machines. In his reminiscence, he bought our house quickly thanks to this business. Even though he had just a short period with it, the trading was good enough to keep the family thriving for a while.

They would endure the hardship until they could not do it anymore. My grandfather started to go out more often in the morning and even he came back home within the same morning. He had changed his course of heart. He cheated on my grandmother several times even meanwhile she was carrying their eighth child – my youngest aunt. They broke, financially and emotionally. Eventually, they established a "normalcy" – stayed separately from each other's business while keeping living under the same roof.

When I grew up, I would see them fight each other once in a while then more often, and in such a barbaric way that until some point, I could not bear to witness any longer. I was forced to be the one who remained in the middle of everything. I was "trained" to endure and witness cruelty, some other times I found myself listening to mundane conflicts between them in a stoical way due to the fact I had become too familiar with them.

After my father's father-in-law left, my grandparents would start to criticize each other. My grandma complained my grandpa indulged his son too much when he was younger then in return, he blamed her for "all of this" happening as she did not agree to the marriage between my parents... Here is the truth, my parents never got married, I was born and registered as a daughter of my father and a daughter of my mother in the meantime they did not commit any legal terms to each other which is quite rare back then in Vietnam.

I found out about this truth and accepted it as a part of my life without any surprise. Have I ever been surprised about life? The answer is yes. At how cruel it may turn out to be and also how blessing it may bring forth. However, it did not matter whether I accepted it or not, all I felt was a persistent, lingering loneliness that seemed to perpetually haunt my life.

Especially since I reached the age of fourteen, I began to experience the intertwining melancholy and profound sorrow with the relentless emergence of depressive episodes, then the chronic migraine would follow afterward. I intended to stay alone and be away from everybody else. I did not find any strong connection that I could lean on except music, reading, and writing journals. Studying was simply a load that I must keep up with and carry on so I would not lose my scholarship.

Well as I mentioned, I did claim the first rank in my secondary school class for four years and gained a few rewards in Biology. I was recognized as the student who grew up with grandparents as one's patron in a poor economical situation, hence for the financial support from the Ward People's Committee in the period of three summer months after secondary school. On the other hand, if I could score well and study in an advanced high school, they would keep supporting me for the next three years until I got eighteen.

I had a stable fixed job, working as a waitress in an Italian restaurant after graduating from secondary school and waiting for my exam result.

In Vietnam, high school and University entrance exams, then studying ranking are obviously the hottest news every summer. We would run for excellent titles and compete with each other ever since primary school in order to attend the best schools in town. Parents will invest a ton of money and time to bring their children to this kind of "extracurricular" class which will vary in different main subjects. In our country, there is only one way to go up and gain a stand in this society, to study and study well.

I registered myself to the two most difficult high schools in town and not under anyone's instruction. My study was hardly up to debate. It had been my own business ever since I was a kid. I got my confidence and pride. I did my best or probably not.

My dream was to keep studying biology with an excellent education. I dreamt to be an environmentalist, a biologist who would study flora and fauna as much as I want.

On a summer afternoon, I remember I was preparing for the working shift when a colleague who worked in the kitchen and was still young and already a sophomore, approached me. She handed me a local newspaper and informed me that the national exam results had just been announced this very same afternoon. She advised me to call and check for the results. I remember the bloody blood rushing through my veins to my head, my heart was beating just as loud as the boiling pasta pot in the kitchen. The sun hit my skin a bit more intensely that afternoon... Everybody was looking at me while I was calling an automatic agency through the phone. I pressed my contest registered codes, answered my birthday then waited. My marks were great but then I failed the most excellent high school though I got myself to the second best. I did not understand why everybody was cheering me up. Well, I did pass the other one but my dream, they could not understand. By the way, I had never shared with anyone about my silly dream of being an environmentalist. In Vietnam? I was merely a dreamer. And here still I am.

I could not help but feel a sense of guilt as I had let myself down, along with those who had been there to support me in pursuing my goals. I particularly felt remorseful towards D.'s father, who had taken the time to drive both D. and me to a far-off examination center, only for me to fall short although I knew that he would never harbor such feelings towards my outcome. The presence of D.'s family in my life had always been cherished and deeply meaningful. They were dear individuals who serendipitously entered my inner world in the most significant of ways.

I heard that D. passed the entrance exam and she was going to study in an advanced class in Literature where she would prepare to be a journalist or a reporter. She was on the way to her dream. I was happy for her and at the same time, I felt like our connection would become more distant because of this. I felt insecure as I could not make it to the same high school as she did. The rest of the summer was supposed to be great as I just turned fifteen that March and was about to enter a new chapter in my adolescent years yet who cares? I did not make enough money to tailor a new set of Ao Dai even. Right, I was expected to be excited to wear Ao Dai as the national obligatory uniform for female teachers and female high school students at last. Notwithstanding, I was upset and feeling poor in my spirit.

I still remember there were several menstrual periods in which I did not even have enough money to buy sanitary pads. Indeed those were such difficult times in my life, just like my grandparents's relationship, economically and emotionally. I saw the hardship in maintaining even just daily meals in my family which had only the three of us living together. There would be days I might have lunch with my grandfather and on other ones when I did not have to go to work, I would dine with my grandmother. My youngest aunt had gone and worked for one of my uncles in Saigon a few years before I entered high school. Hence I was the only one who had to do little daily tasks and help my grandparents when in need.

Quite often I was strangled while following their clashing ideas and fulfilling their endless little tasks every day. My grandmother would complain that I did the task the "other" assigned me first and ignore hers and vice versa. My grandfather remained silent or shared with me such bitter and cold looks. Then whenever my aunts came to visit them or during conversations on the phone with my uncles who were living and working in Saigon, they would talk badly about each other, and about how stubborn and disrespectful I was. My grandparents had been fighting more often ever since I was in my secondary school years. They were blaming me for not doing housework and then in the summer before studying in high school, for going home late from the night shift. My oldest aunt would ask me such questions once about why I kept working and making them worried. I did not answer yet I just wanted to scream out loud that if I did not work, who would pay for my studying and personal expenses and then my extracurricular classes?

I found myself incredibly fragile, unable to shield myself from the weight of thoughtless words and the lingering "shadows" of constant gloom. It was at the tender age of fourteen that I abruptly realized I stood before an immense, expansive world all on my own. It was this realization that sparked the idea of seeking a part-time job, a growing step towards self-sufficiency and empowerment.

My first year in high school was essentially tough if I had not described it as the total absence of an innocence age. I was at the peak of those depressed episodes, during that time I had to run or hustle to the bathroom so no one could see me crying. My emotions were sporadically up then down, and fluctuating between a pinnacle of positivity and feeling almost nothing.
It happened once then twice then every single day a week. I could not turn to anyone or anything to cover this deeply injured spirit being cocktailed with such turbulent hormone control. I barely focused on studying but still tried remaining to be "sane" while working hard every day after school time. I would ride my bicycle with my sweaty ao dai to the restaurant, where I would swiftly change into a comfortable t-shirt and slip into a pair of jeans that I had carefully packed in another bag before going to school, work till ten thirty at night then try to do my homework until late. I maintained this routine until after Lunar New Year's Eve or the so-called Tet in

Vietnam. Meanwhile I was discretely planning a project and could not wait any longer to start it.

During the last couple of months before completing the first year in high school, I came up with a plan. I stopped being upset and started to think clearly and save as much money as I could. I am never sure for how long I wanted to run away, yet I know it had been there before I could recognize its presence forming in my mind. Together with my savings, I would borrow most of my "escape" money from a dear neighbor.

P. shared a lovely part of my childhood as we lived in the same alley and right in front of each other's house. She was living with her grandparents as I was too. She is six years older than me but somewhat friendship is not defined by age but by such a common situation we share. Her mother abandoned her when she was just born after a few weeks. She left the little baby to aunt H. who happened to play around our house's front yard, and walked away. My oldest aunt was shocked as she was left to her own device with a tiny creature who just kept crying for her mother. She ended up crying and calling my grandma. P.'s grandmother was running to all of them when she recognized P's cry. Since that time P. grew up in the same house and her father would come to visit every day. Why he would not take care of her in the same house I never wonder as neither I do in my own case.

P. went to work with her uncle in Laos, met her later ex-husband, and at the beginning she was prohibited by her family to keep seeing him again. However, the couple insisted on getting married as she already got pregnant for four months. I could remember this period of our shared sentiment, a bit lost yet feeling like the world could be our oyster if we stuck together and supported each other no matter where we might be.

She said me to not bother about the money and I could return to her anytime. She also said probably she would not be able to see me again, she would have to live in the North for a while after the wedding. I had not returned that money until ten years later.

As the fact P. was the only one who knew about my plan, I asked her another favor to hide my luggage. Her grandparents did not see or pay attention to her sneaky action when she slipped the large black luggage under her bed that day. I bought this one with my savings money, a huge enough luggage to carry a few important books, clothes, a couple of pairs of shoes and sandals, and my favorite canvas print with the Sesshoumaru character under the magical moonlight because it always brought me peace to look at, a paper version of the only Cambridge English dictionary I bought the year before, and an old Discman Sony Walkman[17] – the model that one can not find it anymore even in the black market for the reason that my father already got it in a thrift market in Sai Gon, and probably had been exchanged through many hands for a lot of time.

I went to buy a train ticket only one day before I was going to leave and one day after my first high school year graduation event. I do not recall which book I was reading at the time, probably a romantic adventurous novel or a philosophical book yet for children from one of my favorite Vietnamese authors – *Nguyen Ngoc Thuan*. I quoted a lot of his sayings due to this period but somehow they just made me feel

---

17   A portable CD player from Sony.

more sad and depressed so I stopped reading his book after a while. Books and music at that moment were the two elements that can affect my fundamental ideas and philosophical motivations, and such effective catalysts to my emotional world in real time.

I woke up at three forty-five on Saturday morning – the first weekend of the summer break. My grandfather caught me brushing my teeth quite early, and gently he asked why I did not sleep some more, I had the whole summer ahead to rest. During summertime in Vietnam, dawn comes around five and daytime can last within the next fourteen hours at its peak in June. It was the thirty-first of May in 2010. I responded quickly without any stirring emotion in my voice, "I am going for a run now", and for an instant I felt extremely guilty to know that my grandfather, in any aspect, still cared for me as his little granddaughter and here I was, scheming to leave him and lying to him like that.
But I had to leave no matter the cost, I thought to myself because they would keep fighting and I would keep suffering from this mundane violence.

All I thought about was that I had got a ticket and an early train to catch, then I would have a whole summer from the South calling for me, a full of adventure and freedom summer ahead of me... oh how innocent I was and how rebellious I might become when I was sixteen.

I had walked the same old route numerous times between my house and the local secondary school, which also opened to the main road, and yet that time felt different. It all began to become vague in my reminiscence, even I remember that the alley somehow became wider, the air was lighter with the cheerful summer vibe painted in everything I saw, and surely the sky that morning was beautifully higher, serene, and sadly blue. I felt scared, I felt excited, and I felt lonely all at the same time.

VI.

The working and freedom tale

The permissible working age in Vietnam is probably like everywhere else in the world, must be above eighteen years old. However, if minor children are under presentation and agreement from their parents or patron with an agreement and suitable salary negotiation from employers, from sixteen years old, a young adolescent can work and earn legally.

In the previous summer, I went to work in a local Italian restaurant which was also one of the only two Italian restaurants in town, I had to ask my youngest aunt to bring me there and talk with the manager. I heard her tell us one time about the night she dined out with her newlywed husband's family at this restaurant. It was an impressive and luxurious experience to dine with all sorts of "dainty" and well-prepared dishes, excellent enough that when I listened to her little story, all I wanted was to be able to work and practice speaking English in such a place.

As I was just fifteen that summer, the challenge of getting hired became even more daunting. However, I managed to convince my aunt to accompany me and vouch for my capabilities, assuring the manager that I would give my utmost dedication and responsibility, and my aunt would take responsibility under any circumstances. To my delight, the manager granted my request and agreed to let me join the team.

It was not as easy as I imagined. Literally being a waitress is a hard job no matter in whatever kind of fancy café or luxury restaurant one is recruited for. The more lavish it is, the harder and better one is required to deliver. In reminiscence, I brought this challenge to myself as I have always done. I wanted to earn money so hard as it was the prior motivation yet to escape from my current living condition and "indulge" myself in such hardship was another idea. I never forget those late summer nights of going home and enjoying such a beautiful breeze blowing from another direction, and at that moment I felt somehow freedom was something one could achieve if one works hard enough.

The idea of looking for freedom has been sown since I was a child. In those summer days when I could spend leisure time wandering around my areas, searching for new alleys and new routes going back and forth home besides the one I took to the local schools, I would do it alone or ask my cousins to join me. In some cases, I joined the search with my neighbor friends. We never got bored at it but I was the only one who probably seldom felt tired of walking and wandering like that. I went wild for some time and did not go home until after lunchtime, even though I knew I might be scolded or threatened to spank which scared me most.

There was one day I found a new alley leading to the main road that connects to other main roads of the city. This was incredible to me. I called anyone around me be it, my neighbors or cousins, to follow me to this new route and I would make up such a hilarious ritual. There would be a little nice "plaza" out of nowhere before leading us to the main road, so from there, I would shout "freedom" as loud as possible while running toward the main road. I asked people to follow me and we would keep repeating doing the same things then laughed at ourselves really hard as if nothing else matted but this very nonsense moment we shared together. Later on, I discover that it was one of the closest alleys for walking to my secondary school. The innocent chapter also closed when we all went to secondary schools. Yet I never stopped amazing myself with those sorts of "brainstorming" ideas of looking for such freedom even until now.

A familiar feeling ran down my guts when I was dragging my luggage through the small alley on that early summer morning in May.
I said to myself I would save every single dime from that on in order to survive yet I was so afraid someone might catch me in a hurry from running away, I had to call a taxi as soon as I reached the other end of the alley to the main road.
In Vietnam existing such a service called "xe om" for ever long time before. Instead of ordering a taxi, one would catch a biker at a cheaper price and they would bring you through any small narrow alleys

without a single trouble. The only problem that remained was they would not always be in your eyesight. Hence you had to wait or either way, call their personal contact. I did not go for either way because I thought the local biker would be there as always. As this same local biker happened to know my grandmother as he drove her to the downtown market for the last ten years and one should make sure that no other people knew about her "whereabouts".

I prayed he would not be there at the end of the alley that morning. I kept praying and walking... Until I saw a taxi already waiting by the end of the alley, quickly hopped in the taxi without looking around, the hand that was holding my worn-out Nokia 1100, full of sweat and shaking. And I just realized freedom could cost you a little peace of mind.

The very first money I earned in my life was not actually from working in the Italian restaurant as one may be able to figure out. It was actually from selling those "self-made" comics with D., through a period of lending my own comics to my neighbors and classmates, selling handcraft season greeting cards and silly printed keychains, etc. There was a time I would trade my neighbor's drawings for one thousand dongs each and sell them again to my classmates with different amounts of profit.

There was one time in the fourteenth summer, I and my other two close friends who are actually twin sisters as well as my neighbors then with one more person who was a classmate of the twins, all together we came to an education center and asked to work as leaflet distributors. I can not recall who came up with this idea first but I bet it might have been me.

We had to come to the education centre at that same time every day, receive about two hundred leaflets each, make sure to spread them well according to the indicated areas as the agency would go check as they threatened, and come back within the next four hours. The deal was that we would receive money every single workday.

Then one of us, the classmate, gave up after the first day after munching and drinking all of the snacks and water she brought along. The three of us stood tall and kept wandering around for four hours every day until the fourth day. We took our courage to ask for the job "escape". Due to the fact that the sun hit too harshly plus the monotonous character of such a job, we had to agree that we all missed our cool room at home and we did not need money that hard. Yet we wanted our righteous payment as they had not given us any dime. They made a solid excuse that we did not finish working at least for a month so they would not be able to pay us as promised.

We were not as "beefy" and courageous as in the beginning when we went to ask for a job. With sullen eyes and sulking voices, we went to the twin's house and kept talking for a while until their mother came home from a work break. I spent quite a handful of time at their house, doing homework with the twin and having lunch with their family. I really like their parents and have always seen them as my close relatives. And then after that time, I would feel even more tied to them even though the connection became vague fast after as we had to attend different high schools.

The mother detected such a subnormal ambiance when she entered the house. Without any difficulty, she figured out there might be something wrong with the part-time job and asked us if everything were alright. We told her everything and expected her to react to what had happened like she might scold us for being lazy or even worse, being such chicken about our circumstances. But no not at all as what we had told each other, apparently she was taking us under her wings and briefly coming to a solution – brought us all to that education center and started to "educate" them in return about how to treat young labors. She was so cool that I wish I could have parents like theirs, as well as D.'s, and my cousins's... Finally, we got our money. Eventhough I would consider this as the very first salary in my life, it had been rather a life lesson about how to deal with all kinds of adult greed.

Working from a young age brings one unexpected and eye-opening experiences. One just needs to be more careful about that young adolescent sorrow, it might eat one alive anytime. I could see it from my grandfather then my father and anyone that I come across on the road.

In that same summer when I worked in the Italian restaurant, I had learned much more than I was supposed to do. After a couple of months of working consecutively, I started to feel more confident and accustomed to the routine, my coworkers, the environment, and whatever types of customers we might see every day.

Thereupon I came across a weird situation, that another waitress and the only cashier in the restaurant had experienced at the same time. On a fine afternoon, I was looking at the restaurant owner's CD collections we had there by the cashier counter, and about to decide which artist's album I would choose to play first. The manager came close relaxingly and asked me about how I was doing with the job in general. Without any suspicion, I simply said I was learning a lot from H. and T., my other coworkers, and really thankful for the opportunity. He smiled gently then dropped an abrupt comment that he wished he could have someone like me to accompany him for a date. At that instant, I was completely astonished. I had just seen his daughter visit us the other day and was exactly the same as my age.

I felt obscene and confused, yet I took my courage to say only one thing, "you should have not said that to me. I am just about your daughter's age" and then left.

My colleagues were even more surprised by my reaction and from that point, I could notice that we stuck closer to each other. We did not see the manager come to the restaurant for several days afterward. Then suddenly he appeared again and showed up to be more aggressively aware of his position. He would urge us to be more hurried in serving customers or more professional in dealing with certain situations. My colleagues and I simply exchanged silent signals and covered each other's shift to eating really fast. I heard one of the colleagues got harassed even worse because he kept calling her after working time. She quit the job not long before I did the next year.

I never told such kind of stories to anyone, especially my family. I had always thought that hey would simply not understand and even started to blame me for insisting to work. Neither I told them about what happened with the education center. I even hid from them the fact I went to work as a leaflet distributor as I was afraid that my grandparents would not let me do it. For certain they might give me a lecture and force me to stay home.

When I was in primary school, freedom to me without any adornment would be days of wandering around our local area and did not have to go to school, do homework or spend time for napping, and being able to save pocket money to buy comics and share it with friends. During the period of the last two years of secondary school and high school, I was obsessed with business ideas and being able to earn good money, then having a place of my own and starting to build my career.

When I had already worked for a few years, I dreamed of travelling and establishing my career in a brandnew way. I wanted to earn money from my passion for the thing I love to do. Freedom would not come in a practical way anymore. At the time it should be poetic and amusing through travelling, writing, being loved back or being rejected. Eventually, I come up with a new meaning of freedom, it must be traded with a purpose, a living goal, and someone else's dream. I realize that all of these objects I had ever chased after, were simply a distracted mind from a wiser insight. Real freedom must come from owning one's own privacy. I simply wandered around in order to search for what I have even though did not own it.

Do we really own freedom though?

Looking back thoughtfully no one had ever asked me to go out and earn money from an early age. Yet I could wake up and listen to the birds chirping, people chatting, the nearby café music playing, and all I could feel was another day I must not let it out – the will to run away from that lonely place. If someone did not want to take you under their wings anymore, they would not be content about doing it, right? Firstly, both of my older aunts did just like that. They refused to keep going on supporting me, and said to me directly, "you should call your father since now on." They too had children and I just thought to myself who I was though in comparison with theirs?

Sometimes I could overhear through a conversation between my grandmother and my aunt H. about me as if I were an inevitable burden which they must carry. "If you can not do it anymore, call her father to bring her back to the south.[18]" Aunt H. said, my

---

18   Meaning Saigon.

grandmother kept complaining until that point but then she remained silent.

There had just been always a big question dangling from my head and torturing my heart, who would be there for me if I really need someone? I thought money might help me answer the riddle yet it only opens a passage to different ones.

VII.

What happened in Saigon? Part Two

It all came up with a plan but was mostly impulsive. I had hesitated to write down this part due to a fact that is relative to an acquaintance whom all I knew was simply through an online website named after the infamous book series, *Harry Potter*. She was an active and friendly admin in our online community. She was "categorized" into *Slytherin* and sounded quite a strong personality and also one of the most beautiful people I have ever met. We called her "*Six*" as her user nickname on *HarryPotter.vn* or as known under the acronym HPVN, *Harry Potter Vietnam Network*.

I was not as much an active member as others except when it came to the *House Cup Thesis* period, I would contribute to my house which was *Hufflepuff* by submitting quality essays or earning points through Fan Fiction stories. Therefore the nickname *"winedarksea"*[19] had been online solely around *Hufflepuff Common Room, Remembrall* or as I mentioned above, *House Cup Thesis*. I encountered Six on the *Common Room* "chat box" several times and I was the one who inboxed her directly.

As I quickly realized that I could join HPVN offline meetings in Saigon next summer, I came up with the proposal to stay with her for a short term before looking for a place on my own. After exchanging a few conversations with Six, she agreed only with the condition that she would not be able to show me around that much hence I had to take care of myself while staying there.

This news warmed my heart a thousand times, resulting in me becoming more excited every day as the summer approached. I woke up and realized I had a plan, a project, a path of my own. At that time I understood how one is driven by one's life goal even in perspective that life goal seemed obviously imprudent and foolish.

---

19 These are not real nicknames at least in this case. The author would like to keep the privacy of forum members.

Not only stopped at that but Six would also keep checking me out during my train trip to Saigon. She asked me if I prepared everything well, if had I arrived safe and sound, and if had anyone come to pick me up after. I said to her almost everything except the part I ran away from my family in Da Nang hence I would not ask for my father's help.

She quickly replied, "I will come to pick you up."

I still vividly recall Saigon ambiance as we journeyed from the Central Train Station to District 12, where Six and her younger sister were living at the time. The train trip had taken a full day, and I finally arrived at the early hour of five-thirty in the morning, exhausted from the eventful journey as the period happened as well.

As I stepped off the train, I caught sight of Six eagerly awaiting my arrival, her helmet still on her head, and another one held in her hand, ready for me. Without hesitation, she swiftly helped me and my luggage onto her nimble motorbike, effortlessly navigating through the crisp, untainted morning air, untouched by the usual traffic smoke and noise pollution.

We embarked on a smooth ride towards the tranquil road where the sun was beginning to paint the sky impressively with hues of an early summer morning in Saigon. In that moment, a sense of renewal washed over me, a new chapter unfolding before my eyes.

Six lived with her younger sister in a small but comfortable renting place. It had an attic that was converted to be their bedroom and working place, a narrow concrete counter as the kitchen beside a single bathroom, and the rest of the place would be used as a living room or simply where they could park their motorbikes at night. Her younger sister was also really friendly and got me in her company quite fast just as I did. Though we did not exchange many conversations during that first and also the only week I was there.
They both were busy. Six was working already and her younger sister was still attending university as a senior. There was one time while talking about each other's family, Six shared with me her secret and told me not to report it to her grandmother as if I would have any chance to see her. Just a couple of months before she dropped out of university in order to take care of herself and the younger sister. This was her own decision and she kept lying to her sister about

this fact too. Even though their grandmother who was living in Poland, would send them a bit of money to assist the situation once in a while but it was never enough. Her mother passed away because of cancer seven years ago at the time she told me. Tragically her father hung himself one year later due to a huge debt he could not cope with anymore, leaving the sisters to survive on their own in Saigon.

I listened to her carefully without realizing that I let that sorrow absorb my mind. A sorrowful mind is either a poetic place or a dangerous one.

There I stayed with Six for a week before my father started to call me incessantly. Eventually, as I did not catch them, he did it way much more intensively, then even threatened to ask Interpol to intercede in the case instead. I was in a bookstore on Nguyen Hue st while answering his message for the first time since I left Da Nang.

Finally I agreed to come live with my uncle H. meanwhile I was trying to look for a job nearby.

When I left Six's place, neither of the sisters was at home. I simply texted her that I was leaving, and my father came to help me with the luggage. I would never forget her friendliness, her grand help and hospitality in those days. She said to me to take care, "you sounded like you were lost, how I cannot try to adopt you?"

Then came the day I joined the first offline meeting, it was at a café I would never remember where it was exactly. Another member of HPVN called *littleprince* came to pick me up and drove me to the rendezvous. We were having a fun time while discussing how we would plan a one-night trip to the south east region of the Mekong Delta. I did not see Six anymore the same summer.

About me, after the offline event, I was busy working throughout the summer and left Saigon in hurry as the terrible event happened later on.

I never thought that would be the last time I could see Six. Exactly seven years later with ups-and-downs in my life, I received the news that Six passed away because of the same type of cancer as her mother's. The news came exactly the same period in which Hoi An got a severe flood in late 2017. I wondered whether she remembered me as a strange teenage girl who came to live with her in one summer day, even in a fraction of second during her last minute between life and death.

Little did I know that it was the summer my Little Uncle passed away because of cancer. My father announced about his death later on, in the same summer I tried to escape under the ignorance of the event as if there were something within me urging to be present for the farewell, without knowing what was that exactly.

This tragic event struck my maternal side shockingly as my uncle, the youngest member of the family, was only twenty-seven years old when he departed from us. In those tender moments before his funeral, surrounded by unfamiliar yet supposedly related faces, I found myself in a state of both bewilderment and unexpected serenity. When my father told me that it was time to leave, I chose to be there with them for the last night. In the next morning, we hopped on a funeral bus that brought all of us to the funeral home and we had him cremated according to the Chinese culture just like that.

I have to say that summer was one of the most memorable ones in my life. Because I was happy? Indeed I was. As well as I was thrown into a dark period of my mental health. I experienced such swings of emotion and mood intertwined with the gradual eventful months. There came such episodes of migraine and negative mood battling around my reality and my definition of reality. I would abuse caffeine or sleep as much as I could in order to beat off those episodes. Though I tried to act normally, I was hiding a lot of untold feelings under those smiles.

Finally, I got a full-time job in a bubble milk tea shop near my uncle's house as I had mentioned before. I walked twice times a day and spent my whole summer there when I looked back. The job was monotonous and boring. I had to come at eight o'clock in the morning, clean the floor, arrange and clean these wooden colorful tables and little square mattresses going along with each table, and dust off them well. Then I would wait for customers who were mostly children, teenagers or families with kids.

The shop was founded by a young girl who went to study in Taiwan for a couple of years. She also worked in a bubble tea shop and learned how to do it by the same period. She dropped out of the university after learning all processes of setting up the bubble tea business, asked her mother for funding and joining the shop too. I could recall their non-stop arguments as the mother was not entirely content with the fact her daughter dropped out of the university and became a bubble tea shop owner. One time the mother was peeling a type of zucchini and all of a sudden, she would be eager to launch a big knife at where her daughter sat, and I was nearby. Obviously I was thrilled. The older brother told me to go take a nap meanwhile the heat was there. This brother worked with us during the summer as a parking guard. He had a large tall patio umbrella and a lounge chair right beside it for resting or playing with his *Nintendo* on the pavement.

Even though I did not have a close relationship with any of these people, I maintained a good enough job in order to have free bubble milk tea every night. The moment I realized that I got a bit chubby, I had to say no to this ritual. The reason that I had more chances to talk with the mother than anyone else, would be because I saw her being busy arranging and cleaning something all of the time while the daughter was serving bubble tea, being somewhere else or looking at the phone, and I felt bad about that. I would ask her if she needed my help to assist in the kitchen but she would shake her head and say fine.

After boiling two huge pots of tea and bubbles and might be more, the mother started to cook the meal for us and repeated the same routine every morning.

Then gradually they invested to buy a two-case fridge, filled with super good and expensive ice creams and colorful syrups. I was one of the fans of those expensive ice creams. The last time I had one of those, I was walking home in the rain and crying while trying to finish it. I felt miserable all of a sudden and the taste quickly turned vague. I did not buy ice cream anymore since I wanted to save it for getting a train ticket back to Da Nang.

One time I recall, there was a teenage girl who appeared with a cold looking man and about average age. He did not order anything nor talk with her. She was, in contrast, genuinely amicable and quite outgoing. I had her order and was about to leave the table, she called me back and asked if I could stay there and chat with her while the shop was not really crowded, if not saying totally deserted on such a rainy summer night. Maybe that was the reason they chose to stop by our tea shop. All of a sudden she wanted to know whether she looked like a famous singer and actress. I said no, not really. Then immediately she continued, "do you believe that I am Q.A's younger sister?" I paused for a bit, tried not to laugh, and shrugged my shoulders, "possibly".

I asked her that I must leave the table as I had to attend to other customers who just stepped in. About ten minutes later, the teenage girl left with the cold man to a black car waiting right in front of the shop. This man did not say a word even during our brief awkward conversation. On the other hand, the girl did not even touch her boba milk tea. Later on, I found out through the internet that she is indeed a famous singer's sister.

After two months of working in this shop, the said accident with me and my father happened, I was upset and turned into a deeply wounded state where I could not go to work anymore. I did not feel like seeing people let alone smiling with customers and asking them what kind of milk tea they might want that day.

My father called me the next day as if nothing had ever happened and suggested to me that I could move in to live with his family in Saigon. He could help me register to study at a local high school. I was amazed and smirked at the fact that he never knew how hard it was for me to pass the entrance exam to the high school in Da Nang. It was not any random high school that one can register at, for that it took a hard deal of time, effort and a stressed-out period to get into.

I was ready to leave the city, I thought. Of course, I refused his suggestion but never suspected the growing stoic "person" in my voice.

I hesitated to ask him why he did such things to me yesterday but as I had never felt connected to him, no matter how many times I had wondered the reason, I just let it go or maybe I never do.

My father did not drive me to the train station as well as many times later in our life, he never wanted to say goodbye in such places nor asked me to. He said between us, we do not really need it, I recalled one time he said that while departing at a restaurant before I took the flight back to Europe.

It was my uncle H. who helped me do everything then. I did not think that I would come back to his house again while working with his wife three years later.

VIII.

Then the darkness monster came

Before leaving for the south, I left my family a long handwritten letter in which I would say the truth about what I felt, truly felt. In fact, that was the first time I broke all of the conventional ways in our family, stepped up, showed my emotions, and started to communicate through "words". Furthermore, I said I cared for every single one, every "little family" and loved everybody to my heart, yet I must leave. Then I mentioned each of my aunt's family members' names and sent them personal messages. In the end, it was a four-page A4 length letter therefore I had enough "time and space" to express myself thoroughly. I asked P. to bring this letter to my family the day I left, yes I know, it sounded like a little drama nevertheless I am still glad I did it.
I never asked how my grandparents acknowledged the fact that I ran away from them that summer and kept avoiding seeing them for the rest of the year. It was that I just hoped they might change and respect

each other in their older days. I was still too innocent even after all that I had ever experienced.

Well, a little pain whittling here and there and I did not realize it until my world turned spiky, ugly, and failed.

Even up till now, I could not process the event as something mental specifically rather than an existential crisis nor would I think otherwise about it. I had no knowledge, no help, and no mental assistance in the spoken respect. Later on I tried to look for a clue why it might be the reason for the final decision, and everything turned out to be a possible one. I remember the dangling idea I got through the day about my presence, and it sounded cruelly true to me when I believed that I was a burden to everyone.

The escape did not change anything but myself. The family was rife with unresolved trauma at its core. It did not matter how dramatic the letter and my escape might sound, the stark unraveling character of the event could not speak up for anyone's pain but myself. Sometimes I thought that I was selfish, and again I was a young person who tried to figure out what might be next, own up to my responsibility, and still got lost after all.

Thanks to the help from a neighbor, R. who sold me those cheap drawings and I would sell them again to my classmates in those days, I found a little room in the center. I still remember he told my cousin T., "do not ever do something like your cousin. Chi is insane. I just helped her but I do not think this is a good idea." I was there to see them when he shared his thoughts with us honestly after the whole summer away from Danang. They both dated each other for some time a few years later and separated in the same year.

I did not move directly to my grandparents' house as I realized that nothing had ever changed. Over and above that I felt like our relationship was on edge despite the breakthrough of my behavior and action. I kept searching for a new job while waiting to enter the school day.
On one of those sunny mornings, I cycled through Bach Dang St and noticed that there was a new

restaurant and bar in town. It looked like it had all of the taste in this world from the black and white background to the minimalist ambiance, quite in contrast to anything I had ever seen before in interior decor. Most importantly they were also looking for waiters, waitresses, cooks, and bartenders.

I walked in with confidence notwithstanding I thought that I might look like a lost person who stopped by for a cup of water. A waitress saluted me and asked what I would like to order. I shook my head and replied that I wanted to apply for a part-time job. She asked me to wait there, she would call her boss in this respect.

A young, skinny but full-of-energy foreign man approached me. He looked at me and asked if I had any experience in any of the listing positions. I answered yes, nine months as a waitress at Mr. Pizza restaurant however I wanted to apply for bartender this time. "How old are you?" He asked me in English[20]. "About sixteen years old. Will be seventeen

---

20 The co-founder is a foreign man who found his business in Da Nang, spoke in english in this context.

next March." He immediately shook his head. "No, we can not let minor people serve alcohol. Sorry about this."

I nodded and showed him my respect towards the information. In the meantime, I picked a business card on the ivory white marble counter before walking out to my bicycle, just in case... It was a simple white themed card with elegant black printed word font. On one side it said *"The Dock"* and on the other, it showed two lines of different phone numbers.

When I arrived at my place, I thought of an idea.

Without thinking twice, I picked the first phone number line and sent an SMS to this one.

"Dear, I was the one who came to ask for a part-time position as bartender. I guarantee I will try my best to learn and work. I am a diligent and honest worker. If there's any problem relative to my age, I will take full responsibility for that. My family will be there to assist me. I am quite in a deadlock situation and I really need the job. I am really thankful if you read and reply to this message. Have a good day."

Though it took me a while to compile the message in English and then as SMS was limited in the number of letters, it cost me two messages to send the whole one, in less than five minutes, my phone vibrated and showed a received message on the screen. E. – the young man who interviewed me the same morning as well as the co-owner of The Dock, texted me back. *"Tomorrow at 4 pm. Wear anything as long as they are long black pants and a white shirt. You can start the training."*
I marvelled at the remarkable coincidence that the first line of phone numbers belonged to none other than E., the very person I had spoken to earlier that very day.
Those were peaceful days before the storm came.

It was immensely exhausted embarking on a new chapter in life, juggling work and studies simultaneously. I was certainly the only minor at The Port hence it added up to the pressure, be it a product of my own perception or a sophisticated interplay of circumstances weaving together to compose such truth. I found myself overwhelmed physically and mentally, and was utterly drained.

E. was a silent and calm man in my reflections. He is from Sweden and was only nine years older than me when he opened The Port together with an Australian partner. He showed me where they had the wine storage, all the kinds and origins of liquors and spirits, and which types of glass I had to use to serve which styles of wine or cocktail. I would stand there in front of the counter and E. would sit there behind the bar, I had to answer him which type of wine he was asking because we had more than ten brands of spirits and eleven brands of wines in the house, show him the type of glass we were going to use to serve a *gimlet*[21] for example.

Things must follow their order and rhythm. If I had to serve a cocktail fast and professionally, I needed to not hesitate in my thinking and movement. I remembered there was one night, the bar was empty and I had to wash all of the glasses and tools we used to practice, unintentionally I broke a wineglass or it was just cracking after a few uses either way. I bled myself and was fairly shocked. At the time I was scared that E. would see me breaking something from

---

21 Gimlet is a classic cocktail featuring gin and lime juice with ratio 1:1.

the bar property yet he did see it. In an instant, he collected the broken glass fragments and threw them in the trash bin, held my wrist, and ran the cut under the water. He said briefly while processing all of those movements in a fraction of a second, "when something is broken, you throw it and do not worry about it anymore." I always remember him this way from then on. A cold, and professional hardworking man, a decisive businessman, and a strict boss.

I got a uniform according to my size after the second day of training. Nevertheless, I could feel the heat from standing behind the counter and being treated as a minor by my coworkers. They were also thinking E. was a bit partial by letting me work there without any experience.

One time E. asked me to make him a classic *mojito*[22] and I did not add mint leaves to the drink! He insisted on knowing why I did not follow the recipe. I was bursting with a bad temper and responded frankly that I remembered every single step, but a coworker who provided the instructions had not given me the correct recipe. That same coworker

---
22 Mojito is a classic highball drink that uses ingredients including rum, lime, mint, and sugar. The mixture is topped off with a little club soda to create a thirst-quenching libation.

calmly replied that he had done his best to show me everything. Clearly I was in a weak situation to cover my fault. E. listened to everyone and shut the conversation simply by saying, *"try better next time,"* and finished his mojito.

I gave up on the fifth day. I texted an apology to E. and said I would come to leave the uniform that afternoon. When I came to return the uniform, he was at another bar two meters from ours. I insisted on bringing the uniform to him and said sorry again. In his look, I could not read many messages but a calm face and word-saving gestures as usual. It was awkward but it was what it was.

Every night I came back to my place from The Port, as the timing of training at the bar and moving to this new stay had aligned, I remember the house owners saving me a humble portion of rice in the rice cooker and soy sauce or ketchup in a small bowl. There were nights I found stir-fried morning glories, fried tofu or stew pork. I was partly a vegetarian, they knew it and hence the preparation. They asked me once if I needed anything else. I said no but still ate the leftover rice almost every night as I remember I always went home with an empty stomach. My part-time job did not offer a meal for sure and even if one of my colleagues asked me to join them, with my pride I would say thanks and withhold.

I rented a small humble room. It had one door connected to the living room and another door worked as a separate entrance through my room to the house. I shared the only bathroom with the family. They were humble working people and quite small even in my memory at the time I was only one meter fifty-six centimeters.

The owners treated me genuinely well as I always remember. They left me a small mattress, a thin blanket, a pillow and some hooks for hanging clothes. Their kids who were seven and three years old, got used to my presence in the house quite fast. Especially the younger one, she would scream my name every time I came home from somewhere and hug me in pure joy or come to my room and I would lend her one earphone to listen to music from my walkman. We stayed quiet for a while then she would leave for lunchtime.

Those days reminded me of when I worked in the bubble tea shop in some ways. As I spent almost twelve hours every day in that shop which was actually the owners' house. I felt like a part of the family too.

However, most of the time, I found myself lying in the embrace of darkness, intentionally narrowing the divide between the world of the little girl and my own. Among my collection of CDs, a farewell gift from an HPVN member named *"littleprince"* awaited— a playlist curated with the works of diverse, gifted composers, the specific details of which have faded from memory. Yet, within this compilation, "Sad Angel" by Igor Krutoy[23] possessed an inexplicable allure that captured my heart completely.

Embedded within the melody lies a depth and darkness far beyond simple sorrow, as if I could envelop myself in the exquisite melancholy woven into each intricately written note upon that humble "napkin."[24] The song, "Sad Angel," became my

---

23 A Ukrainian and Russian music composer, performer, producer and musical promoter. Krutoy was awarded the Lenin Komsomol Prize in 1989.

24 In the song video, the composer was writing music notes on this napkin in the café.

constant companion, its ethereal strains echoing ceaselessly, until it felt as if this singular composition held the power to suffice, encapsulating my desire for the *last* departure within its haunting embrace. Then I kept crying until I felt entirely numbed or asleep.

My aunt, L. came to persuade me to move in with her instead. She said I could accompany her and stay with her newborn son. I agreed as long as I did not have to see my grandparents nor I asked about how they were doing. Simply, I gave up. I did not want to try anymore.

One morning, aunt L. came to my place and talk with the owners, said thanks to them for taking care of me, gave them rental days payment, and drove me to the house of my oldest aunt H. I asked where aunt L.'s husband was, she kept silent until I figured out that they were in a serious quarrel. He sounded drunk or tired or annoyed for some invisible reasons most of the time. He wanted us to come live together as he had found a few good places. He promised my aunt L. that he would not spend money extravagantly anymore and that she did not have to move in with his family from then on. During the period of living together, we had to move around four different places from both sides of the river, and never I did wonder why. I was occupied with an idea in my mind since the time we lived at aunt H.'s house.

I went to pick up a new set of razors at a local grocery store. I would try to harm myself secretly and face the day as if nothing had ever happened. It was a dark dark time of my life and most of the time I used the word "deadlock" in my diary. I had to wear a long-sleeved jacket to cover the injuries on my wrists each time I had physics education class because the uniform was designed with a short sleeves t-shirt.

If the past year I had to run to cry in the school toilet, a year later I would no longer cry. It seemed that I became hypersensitive and experienced PTSD[25] without recognizing the pattern. I would call this period depression or simply, a bad day. Until one day I decided to spend my money on magnesium pills[26].

---

25 Post-traumatic stress disorder (PTSD) is a disorder that develops in some people who have experienced a shocking, scary, or dangerous event, according to National Institutes of Health (.gov).
26 A kind of supplement for body.

Because this kind of medicine casually requires a prescription and I was a minor when I went to ask for it, the pharmacist suspiciously looked at my facial expression and questioned not only the purchasing purpose but also my integrity. I lied to her quite easily even though I felt so bad about it. Indirectly I made her break the Hippocratic Oath[27].

The first night we stayed at the new place after moving out from aunt H.'s house, I took seven magnesium pills at once and thought to myself that I might have to keep overdosing if it was not "enough". I was wrong.

I was awakened by a fierce burn down my throat to the stomach. I could not breathe, "the air must have been drained out *up there*," I thought and was trying to grab as much air as I could. "I *must live*," I announced and demanded clearly to my entire body. Then slowly I made some effort to call my aunt, firstly, no one heard me, the second time, she moved a little, gradually she moved towards me and realized there was something wrong... As I had only enough

---

[27] The Hippocratic Oath is an oath of ethics historically taken by physicians widely known in medical context.

strength to murmur, my aunt had to come closer with her ears, "I need water..." I whispered. My uncle-in-law N. was hurrying with a glass of water to me and asked me what happened. My aunt urged him to dress and bring me to the emergency room no matter what the reasons were, while calling aunt Lo. I made one final effort to point them to the pack of pills besides me before falling into an unconsciousness again.

IX.

The handwritten letters

"Today is..., month, year.

Dear father,

How are you recently?

First of all, I would like to say thanks for your last letter. Everybody here is doing good. I can write the letter on my own now. I will be in third grade soon.

How is mother L.? Please help me say hello to her. I hope the family is doing well.

I will include my drawing with the letter. I tried my best to draw you, mother L., me and brother T. together.

Hope to see you soon,
Your daughter."

When I was six years old, my favorite aunt L. was the one who showed me how to write a hand letter for the first time. One had to mention the date then a respectful greeting, a typical "how are you" and following information about how one was doing. I would never say to anyone about the fact that I enjoy writing a letter much more than the action of sending it to someone. Especially in this case, it was my father and his new family with whom I had yet never met and connected.

Later on, aunt L. came to work with my father as a tailor and a cook in Saigon when my father built a small garment "factory". It was not literally a factory as it might sound. My father would gather a group of "freshmen" including my uncles and teach them to follow the procedure of tailoring windbreaker jackets or suits. My grandfather sometimes helped him look for more people in case they had to run a bulk order in the long term. At other times he had to train the newcomers and let them live at our place. Within this period my father came home several times to bring these apprentices to Saigon in addition he would spend some time with us too. I enjoyed his presence as I always received some new clothes and little gifts or we would go shopping for the new school year.

In some such way, I felt the way people treated me while he was there too – I was a child who has a father and her father was there with her. As simple as I put it yet it is true.

Though both of my parents were not there, I had never thought otherwise rather than accepted their absence and followed my changing daily routine. As a kid as well as an adolescent and then a young adult, I never think about it as something that could decide my life. I did not live up to social norms let alone see myself as an orphan. However, his presence could bring me such strange feelings about having a father. I could not feel connected to him as much as I should have.

After all, he did not attend important moments in my life, and by that time aunt L. and my grandmother were the people who did take care of me the most as his regard. Hence her absence brought me a lot of sadness and I missed her most of the time.

There was one of those times my father came to visit us, he helped me write and send a letter to her. This time when I wrote "I miss you" in the letter, I did feel it. Someone is missing in your life, it was sad and it was beautiful.

The epoch of innocence passes briefly without one's awareness but it would not stop me from writing hand letters once every while. Even the fact that my father gave me back all of the letters and postcards I had ever written for him, did not make me stop doing it at most. It was the year he wanted to cut off contact with me and "harm" himself.
After two months since my father learned that I went to the hospital for an emergency situation, my stepmother at the moment, called me as I mentioned above. He would keep avoiding my calls or even answer with a very strange cold voice in a few single words then abruptly hung the phone. He did not behave better than me in any aspect.

I remember my uncle-in-law, uncle N., was there when a nurse approached us. He passed her the blister pack of pills while was even still confused about the situation in general, and he urged her to check my stomach. The nurse called another doctor and pushed me to a smaller room where they could check my intestine and urine. They said all would be fine. They injected some liquid that would help wipe out all of the magnesium I digested and it was going to affect me within twenty minutes. In the meantime, the nurse set up distilled water mixed with something else which I was not sure about. At that moment, a peculiar sensation enveloped in me, as if my body had become disconnected from my consciousness. A warm stream of heat coursed its way from halfway down my back to my pelvis, and for a brief moment, I thought I was urinating involuntarily. However, as time passed, I came to realize that this was merely a side effect of the anaesthetic injection I had received.

Uncle N. told me to rest and that he would be back soon after buying "banh mi"[28]. I nodded then burst into tears as his presence and care did warm my "frozen" heart for the first time in a long time, then gradually closed my eyes for a while. He carefully left my phone beside me before leaving.

---

28 Banh mi or bánh mì, is a short baguette, consisting of an airy baguette, sour pickled daikon and carrot, crisp cilantro, spicy chilis, and a cool sliver of cucumber surrounding any number of protein options, from sweet minced pork to fatty duck pate or roasted pork char siu.

Uncle N. had always been an impenetrable person to me except one night in my dream he became a monster who took my aunt away. That was the night I cried like pouring rain when I realized since that moment I could not sleep with my aunt L. anymore. Life was cruel to a kid in such a way that the world could be as vertical and pure, and as narrow and limited at the same time.

We had known each other through aunt L. since the time I was still hanging around with them as a little kid. Until they got married and had three children together, I supposed they had not changed the way they see me. I seldom talked much with him but exchanged short and efficient messages with each other even during the time we shared the same roof.

Uncle N. was also the only one who helped me sell away the expensive second-hand scooter which my father bought it for me at the time I got into the university. However, not long after that, circumstances soon took an unexpected turn as my father asked me to sell it because he needed money urgently. My father ventured into the world of new business, risking his hard-earned money in pursuit of his dreams. Unfortunately, luck was not on his side, and he faced challenging times, as he confided in me. However, amidst these tales, there were whispers of another version, suggesting that some of his funds were invested in recreational activities and the company of women. As I felt a mix of sadness and frustration for his behavior, I decided to get rid of it and saved the money to travelling later on.

Somehow uncle N. had been there when one was in need in idiosyncratic situations and for this, one appreciated him as a fair and square, and kind-hearted person.

I was not sure how long I slept there alone yet even after the rest, I did not see anyone in my family around. As I could not bear the hospital scene in the emergency area which was full of accidents and a hectic crowd meandering around sick beds, I marched away without letting the nurse or anyone else know.

Walking along the same road for a few meters, I saw a colorful ice cream shop on the other side. I was fainted and weak yet the vision of sitting on a chair but not a sick bed and enjoying one of those eye-catching combos would be the best deal I could strike to myself. I walked in with confidence even while not carrying money. The first thing I did when I left that traumatic emergency room was to enter an ice cream - coffee shop and order a delicious full-topping ice cream combo in a tall glass. Plainly I did not care about anything anymore.

In spring I moved back to live with my grandparents.

It was dark. Everything was dark around me. I could feel the pitching darkness and at the same time quite "fresh air" in the Universe. I was drifting among it. Was it night or simply was it dark? I was not sure. All I "knew" was that I "was" dying and I could "feel" what it would be like to die, to stay still in the darkness, to not look back, and to forget everything. Instantaneously I heard someone moaning, a distant sound from somewhere below. I could see what was happening "down there". I could see my funeral and everybody was dressed in white linen cloaks and pants as the Vietnamese traditional funeral customs for family. It was aunt L. crying for me. She was crying terribly and looked so sad... I did not want her to be upset like that. I just wanted them to release me as I was everyone's burden, I thought. I started to cry too because I hurt my family a great deal by being "up here" then screamed, "no, do not cry, please, please..."

The dream that happened in the overdosing state

For the trains that will come.

X.

Like a movie but not a destiny

She would go back home from school, said hi to him, and remain silent most of the time. He knew she was experiencing the age of changing – the secondary school with all of those young teenage friends, more difficult homework, and probably soon she would have her first periods. He could not ask her this kind of matter, he knew he should leave it to the grandmother. Oh damn, he did not want to communicate with that woman anymore. Eventhough he wanted to talk with her or even sing her favorite song like the old days especially when he had drunk a few bottles of beer, they were at the edge of their relationship and had been so since a long time ago.

He remembered there was one time when she was about five years old, on a fine summer afternoon he was walking out of the bathroom, and hearing her murmuring according to a familiar voice-over from a

Hong Kong movie in the living room, *"every life is a destiny"*.

He turned his head towards where she was sitting and saw her actually crying. He was feeling half funny half shockingly in front of what he had witnessed. What could this little girl feel when she repeated the deep message and then burst into tears on her own like that? He was wondering and in an instant, he asked her, "why are you crying? No one had done anything to make you cry as such."

"I don't know," just realized her grandfather standing there and catching her in tears all because of an emotional movie scene, she replied with a little embarrassment. "I just felt sad and wanted to cry."

Then quickly he answered, trying to hold his laugh while somehow being serious.

"You don't have to be sad. You have got everything in your life already. Go wash your face, soon we will have dinner." He sounded demanding and strict as he has always been.

Somehow he was right. She was still luckier than those kids who had to go sell lottery from door to door and café to café every single day, she thought to herself.

It was not easy to raise up the kid of one's own son. In this case, it was a girl. He found it a little tricky to be close to her even though he tried. He would show her how to clean the floor, backstitch a hole in worn-out jeans, fix a sewing machine motor or even a loose chain bicycle. In addition to his teaching, he always tried to show them through a practical procedure, first you do this then secondly you do that and she was obligated to pay attention in order to repeat after him. She learned fast though. She also showed her ambition to finish everything as perfectly as possible. In this respect, being perfect would mean following exactly what he had shown. Though quickly her grandmother would scold her for doing things differently from the instructions she gave. It has always been a tug of war since she was aware of the world around her.

They would take naps together in the living room when she was still a kid however, they stopped doing that when she grew up a little more. One day in her first year in primary school, after putting her school bag aside, she took off her top and was about to run to the street. This caught him by surprise and of course, she did not stand a chance to do it. He called her back and started to lecture her that she could not dress like a boy anymore.

"It's not normal for a girl to do like that," he would repeat without explaining what might be the difference between a boy and a girl when they take off their top.

"But it is really hot. It's summer now. You are doing it!" She would insist on knowing the reason with a sulking face.

It took her a while to shake off the mindset of a kid and realize that she had to grow up and become a girl. They had to be alert about this as they had talked with their son another day. "Don't worry. We can take care of her," he never forgot to comfort his son. Meanwhile, her grandmother would complain to him that he was lying and it was her grandmother who had to do almost everything in the house.

Time started to run like disrupted and bluntly repetitive train stops. There were a few precise details here and there but in the whole picture, everything happened swiftly in order to turn into a blurred vision of what one might have about the past. In that scenery of time and space, she never wondered about her mother and had a slight desire to meet her. She could remember when she was about three or four, there would be an intense period where she was taught by her grandmother and the sister of her grandmother that her mother was a villain in her life. She was abandoning her and treating her with a cold heart. She would be taught to answer a kind of yes or no question like an innocent programmed robot. Who would be the bad person and good person between one's mother and father? Then one would answer and repeat it as if one had learned about it by heart for a thousand times, "my mother is a bad person."

She pondered whether this was the reason her family treated her differently from the rest, while her cousins were seen as angels and enjoyed their privileges as carefree kids. They would often call her hurtful names, especially her grandmother, like the futile monkey, the nasty kid, the obnoxious face... However, she also understood that sometimes her personality could be challenging to handle, and like any child growing up, she did not always behave perfectly. Despite this, she could not recall any specific reason why she deserved to be verbally harassed. She once felt deserted because of this, a constant rejection inflicted through her present during her childhood. As if she were a handicapped child in her soul.

A small part of her wondered if her grandmother's possible dislike for Chinese people played a role in the way she treated her, as she carried half of her blood from that heritage. Nevertheless, she wanted to believe that her family's love for her could eventually overcome any prejudices or misunderstandings. Deep down, she knew she was more than just those hurtful labels, and she held on to the hope that they would see her true worth and appreciate her for who she was.

Her heart thus got a constant conflict about how the world was being presented to her when she grew fonder of a set of her own belief in which kindness was the center of it. She started to question her own questions and do what she might feel "right" to do. Then suddenly in the summer she turned eight, her grandmother announced to her that her mother had passed away, the same mother about whom she was taught as a bad one. Once again she was feeling extremely confused. Should she feel miserable about it? In whatever sense a daughter might be taught to feel about her mother's death, a young death as well? None of those made sense to her as one could not be taught to hate or love. It must come from a natural force and connection that which happens between parents and their children.

She did not respond to the event with a single word or show any emotional expressions on her face. Until the day she held the Death Certificate which was passed on to her by her father, she might have felt a thing or two and kept it to herself.

Neither of her grandparents spoke with her in this respect. Her grandmother and almost everyone else who happened to know her, kept looking at her with sad pity faces, as if their sympathy was a means to say they knew what exactly happened to her then and it did matter to whom she actually became. Yet in some certain senses, the way her grandfather treated her or looked at her had been unswerving.

She was officially an orphan, and so once was her grandfather. Two parallel destinies might have come across to this point where one was sharing a common thing with the other. Both she and her grandfather lost their mothers in their young days, and they both were the innocent children of their own destiny.

Maybe he knew how it might feel like to be an orphan and moreover, being seen as an orphan and wishing to be treated as equal as other kids would be.

Yet how uncanny one might find it here that they never actually talk about it together. It might be the distance in their age, the typical discreet manner passing through Vietnamese generations where they would keep their feelings to themselves, or and probably she was too young to talk with. It could be one thousand other reasons why she was never taught to express her feelings genuinely, in the meanwhile, echoing through a part of her childhood, she could hear herself rehearsing the same verse in her mind, *"my mother is a bad person."*

Nevertheless, life is not destiny. If so, our effort and existence would not mean anything. He must have believed in himself to a certain degree so as to walk away from what was built around him. Through so many years, after running away from that little house in a rural village, he seldom looked back and wondered if he had ever done anything unfaithful to his family. Sometimes he told her that he was thankful to himself for deciding to leave and following his own path without letting himself slide sideways.

He would look off into the distance and stay silent. With all of her respect for the silence, she remained still and waited. He did not want to show her his tears for sure. He would be emotional thus the story would be hauled to a chain of questions and comments towards her or certain living advices.

"Have you done your homework?"

"You should wash the dishes and don't let your grandmother grumble about it anymore."

"Every time you go out, bring some money for emergency use, especially now when you start to go to class with the bicycle."

"You have to study well and go to university so no one can give us despite."

"Even though we are a humble family, we should be proud because we work hard and we do not thieve from anyone..."

Then abruptly she said that she would like to become a journalist or "nhà báo" when she grew up after reading a lot of "law and crimes" newspapers. He suddenly laugh, an abrupt one, "you would *báo đời* instead." As a wordplay, informing character in journalism also means a life-ruining party in society or a thug, especially indicating young people.

Certainly, he had her as a little friend until he could not do anymore.

He liked driving his granddaughters on the old bicycle to the city fountain named after a type of local turtle in Da Nang, "baba". The Da Nang Urban Landscape and Environment Force was releasing and nurturing these small tortoises in public, in some hope of changing the city vibe before realizing that people would just go and steal them. Obviously, they stopped doing it after some time.

It was a public recreative area where grass and plants were taken care of, the plaza and pavement were well cleaned, one could see a huge city theatre on the other side of the road, and more interestingly one could go out for a night excursion safely in this area. Her cousin T. and she would hang out together with other kids until their grandfather called them for a night snack like guavas, toasted peanuts or spicy stew snails - a typical street food in Vietnam. When her cousin did not join both of them, he would still drive aunt Lo. and her to the fountain until the tortoises were no longer there. One time, the four of them would drive on the same bicycle together.

On other occasions, they went to take a little walk by the beach after dinner.

About the time they finished paving the pedestrian sidewalk between 2002 and 2004, the construction site had scarcely left these broken bricks and tiles at some corners. She would collect these little pieces and "build" her "house" so only some naughty kids would come and push them back to the ground. She was staying behind the "wall" and had those bricks fall down on her. Even though she ran out of the rumbling scene quickly, it left her with a serious bruise and injury on one foot. He caught this out, reprimanded both the kid and her then they would walk home in silence.

Summertime was her favorite season of the year. In speaking of seasons, the chief feature of Vietnam's weather is diminutive down to two periods, dry and rainy seasons. If one is delighted enough to realize about that, a slight cool breeze in August or a light tone of warm sunshine in March could speak a lot more than its length even just for a swift moment..

Then came summer break when she could go swimming at the beach near their home. In addition to that she did not have to take a nap or solve homework, she had always been a dreamer since then and nothing could interrupt the endless chain of dreams in her mind. It was the perfect season for dreaming. She could keep wandering around the local area where she lived, wondering and living in the imaginary world.

Most of the time she would write about the dream she had got the night before, and keep living with the remnants of them the whole day following. It was a peculiar ability that she could remember her dreams, then let them weave into the landscape of reality. For one time, she met a cute white dog that became a little prince and hung out with her then swiftly turned into the little furry friend again, yet the-whole-night-dream could help her sweep away the invisible fear that the nightmare "monster" had just stormed to her dream during the first few hours of the same sleep.

The mosaic of feelings she had been able to connect to reality, played a significant part in her emotional world. Due to a few single hours of living within the remnants of the dream from the night before, she could sometimes escape reality and become someone else. The main theme of these wonderful dreams would be about becoming a fighter, a warrior, a hero, a survivor who was running away from a monster, a dark force or a typical villain in a chaotic scenario. In another scene, she could fly, jump and climb really fast and or be able to execute magic in this swift and strange journey where her dream brought her in. Therefore, wandering around and letting no one interfere with the realm of a mixed journey where her imagination met her own dream, was one of the favorite parts of her childhood. Until she found out that she could keep the "records" of all of these wonderful worlds by writing them down, she did not hesitate to dive right in and start a brand-new journey. When she turned eight, she began to write her first fiction about a white rabbit's journey which in reality was a toy that got lost and then found by her.

She had often felt a sheer connection between what she saw during the day time and then what she might dream at the same consecutive night. It happened one time, she discovered the fact that up on the ceiling of their old house, existed a secret space where her grandfather used it to store many kinds of stuff and even useless trunks of wood. Then another time, she was mesmerized by seeing her grandfather lifting and dragging from one side to another side a plywood sheet that was supposed to be the ceiling of her grandfather's bedroom, leaving a small square passage as a threshold to the secret hidden "world".

He asked her to give a hand keeping a small stool steady while stacking it up on top of a ladder back chair, and stepping on the other as a ladder, in order to either look for a lost object or constantly storing more old stuffs up in this garret. She would insist to see what might be up there and they would change the role, "be careful, you must hold on the sheet to stay balanced," he reminded her. It turned out that this secret world contained nothing interesting but cobwebs, average-sized wooden pillars which were full of dust and a vast empty space surrounding it.

After seeing this garret, for some curious reasons, her imagination quickly developed a "monster" that kept hiding in this part of the house, suddenly appeared once every while in her nightmare and chased after her as a nagging shadow over her childhood period. Yet even until some time later when she was already in adolescence, this same shadow-monster nightmare kept occurring as a remnant of a long-lost treasure in the same old attic, following a series of dreams within the same night.

Her grandfather then aunt Lo., and she went swimming together several times a week in the summer. Sometimes she would accompany her grandmother and aunt Lo., and almost all the time together with her cousin T. It rarely happened that her grandparents were spotted at the same place. Even when they lived under the same roof, they would have different meals, sleep on different beds, and seldom talk with each other. As they got used to it, it was normalized to take turns hanging out with each of them. Except when they had to celebrate public events like weddings or the annual banquet ceremonies to the ancestors as an important part of Vietnam culture, everybody had to gather and share the same meal. One way or another it was a beautiful time of her childhood when things were as simple as they were without being heated up to the point each of them had to carry traumatic family scars.

There was a period when she had to learn to focus and study in the middle of quarrels day after day then among different members of the family. Once, she witnessed her oldest aunt H. being pushed to the wall by her grandfather as she stepped back in defence and hit the edge, she got a serious bruise on her back arm. Aunt H. was bursting into tears while saying that he could not treat her mother that violently anymore because she had already suffered a lot from him for her whole life. Her grandfather would scream back at both of them, that aunt H. took the side of her grandmother for the fact that they were working together in the same business, and he was simply cut out of the picture like that. It was chaotic.

Eventually, she learned about the family situation, the invisible pressure, and some certain deals between them every time she was back home from school. She felt likely being left out as her grandfather had said about himself, notwithstanding in an extremely distinctive way. Since that period she started to see him as a lone "wolf" acting as if he were completely alone and deeply hurt. She would see him wipe out his tears really fast then keep walking away from her or stay quiet for hours on his old mattress and stare into the distance.

Then he would soon change into a "better" period where he was suddenly becoming more active and robust. He did exercises more frequently and looked likely younger than his actual age. He worked throughout the day, took naps, and went to buy sweet congee more often.

One day he asked her to run for a little grocery task as usual but what she saw when she was back home, was not normal at all. At the passage leading to the kitchen, in the shadow of the late afternoon, she saw him kissing the neighbor woman who was one of their most friendly neighbors. They moved to another area while she kept coming back to run a little business selling sweet congee. She was literally as small as her business, lifted up to his arm while they were trying to make out in the dark, and thought no one could ever know their secret business.

Her heart was racing, and not knowing what else she could do, she hid at the turn of the corner leading to the weird passage as well her grandmother's space. Cringing her body toward the wall, she hoped he would not pay any attention to the possible amount of time it might take to run the task, as she was waiting for the two of them to finish their "business".

Out of nowhere, one of her younger cousins Th. was running toward the kitchen, and probably did see what she had witnessed, quickly getting held back by the arm by her. She looked into her innocent eyes and whispered to her ears, "do not say this to anyone, especially our grandmother," then hugged her really tight as if they could protect each other from all sorts of absurdity in life at that single moment. She was ten years old and her cousin was six by the time. After what she saw, needless to say, she liked her grandfather less and listened to her grandmother more yet without realizing that.

Something had changed in her conscience and the world was getting a little tiny more "polarized" every single day.

Once in a while, there would be a different woman coming to talk with him in the afternoon. This woman could not speak but she was indeed very attractive, and the woman's daughter was her primary school classmate for a year until this friend changed to another class.
After picking her daughter up from the school, they would walk by the house, holding her daughther's hand in her hand, she tried to exchange some information through body language or simply he would pass her a piece of paper with a written message on it. She was way younger than her grandfather but clearly fell for him in all respects. He would ignore her for some time so as to talk again in a "fierce" way. Then she would get angry and not pass by their home anymore. There was some time she pretended to be his client, she would enter their house and he started to have her measured. While no one was there except her again, gradually they slid to his room.

She would try to ignore it and stay only in the living room until they walked out from that.

Despite what the universe had her witnessing, her heart had not changed in the way she felt for her grandfather. She was not born to hate because simply she could not do it. Yet she loved her grandmother even more while having respect for both of them.

Who was exactly left out of the picture though? It was probably either her or all of them.

XI.

In those last summer days

She asked her grandfather if he needed new socks. When she went to gather their laundry, she noticed a few pairs of his socks got holes or were worn out. He shook his head and turned away. They were not in a good relationship, not as good as before. She was so preoccupied with the high school entrance exams, extracurricular classes then a part-time job. She spent her whole day outside until late at night.

As well during the last two years before she entered high school, they often did not share the same meals. He was not even capable of feeding himself economically, he stated the truth. On the other hand, her grandmother would be at the small shop of second-hand clothes with aunt H. on a main street in the center. Somewhat her grandmother was financially able to take care of them both. She would ride her bicycle to this store and share lunch with either of them but most of the time, she had to have a quick meal alone before running to the secondary school.

Nevertheless, this period did not last that long, aunt H. went bankrupt and had to change to a coffee shop business. Her grandmother still kept maintaining the same business at a local market spot close to their home. She started to change her lunch location as her uncle L. vouched to take care of that part and in return, she would help him look after his daughter's homework. Thanks to this time she and her cousin Th. were getting closer, in spite of the fact this little girl was having problems paying attention to whatever matters relative to study, and was quite stubborn the entire time. She would yell at her and they would cry together because she confessed that she felt guilty to do so. She said she really cared for her, all she wanted was the best for her cousin. And they got even tighter after what they witnessed together. She never asked her cousin again if she could still remember what happened that spring afternoon.

In fact, her grandfather would sometimes ask her to join him for lunch or dinner. She or aunt Lo. who had come back from Saigon, would help him go shopping. He might cook or aunt Lo. would cook once, depending on the day, and then divide them into two separate portions, one would be for her uncle L.'s family including her, and another one for the grandfather.

In her family, each of her uncles and aunts took their turn going to work with their brothers in Saigon. Some chose to stay, some wanted to come home, and most of her aunts could only stand for a couple of years before deciding on settling down back home in Da Nang. Except for uncle L. who moved back and forth between both of the cities with his family, every time they reckoned that their economic situation might descend. By the time aunt Lo. was back from Saigon after a year or two working for uncle H., she was asked to help uncle L. with house chores and then assist his wife at an office uniform shop of their own in Da Nang. This lasted in the course of two years until aunt Lo. got married.

There was always one thing she tried to ignore since she started to be aware of their family affair, each of their family members was either having problems with a few other members or in finance. She never wondered whether one problem might lead to another one, yet they seemed to go hand in hand for many years within each "little" family they had created.

One summer day after she graduated from secondary school, she was back from somewhere with a black plastic bag. It was her off day and the summer vacation had not been over until two more weeks. He did not bother whether she was doing fine with the job or how the exam results were going. He was getting old, distracted, and physically more vulnerable. He kept his thoughts to himself more and more as well as her, except her grandmother, she had always spoken plain and straight like ever.

The old house became deteriorated in a severe way at this stage. As if it could speak with one through each and every crevice on the decayed walls, cry through the rooftop loopholes, and even scream out loud every time a good monsoon rain poured down on Earth. Each of the concrete staircase edges in the house was getting worn away, gradually revealing dusty cemented scratches on the dark grey floor, one of them was even showing a fading red patch of a poor random brick.

She always held fond memories of the beginning of each new school year, especially when a neighbor family would visit her grandfather. Blessed with prosperity from their successful business, the father took great delight in dressing his children in new well-tailored uniforms every semester. Enchanted by her grandfather's craftsmanship, these visits evolved into a cherished annual tradition.

Their visits were always accompanied by the most exquisite and high-quality fabrics, which her grandfather skillfully tailored not only for those children as ordered but also for her. He meticulously measured each garment, ensuring that there would be remnants to create her own beautiful uniforms as well. Thanks to this clever action, they were able to go several years without the need to spend money on school uniforms, a secret tradition that continued until she reached high school.

However, the fabric cutting table now was left dismal in a corner, quickly became a thriving and promising land for termites colonies. The sewing machine motor no longer cheered up in the air like before.

As if her grandfather's sickness was partly coming from such dense tight air of his bedroom where he would lie there for days without socializing or even talking. The window was shut, and the curtain was hanging freely on the threshold, warning anyone from stepping into his world. His pain was getting worse each time he figured out something that he thought about hiding it for a while.

The living signal was scarcely there in the old house.

He did not say anything when he found new pairs of socks put nicely on the bed edge. They must be from her. She went to buy them from her first working month's salary. This girl always followed her own ideas no matter what he said or not.
He was suddenly seeing himself a bit emotional.

Her grandfather, once in his life, had to suffer from a serious kidney removal operation as he got overwhelmed by the "unallowable" quantity of pebbles after a long time. He did well for the next ten years until the other kidney got tired as it had to work alone, and started to create these back and waist pains from time to time. Until he saw blood in his urine, he would ask her to buy painkillers and moderate his diet.

These pains came and went away like infinite waves under each season, weather, period of time, and mental health. He carried this turbulent status of an odd relationship with his family and terrible physical health over a period of many years. While he was trying to function with one kidney left, it apparently did not listen to him long after many years of suffering.

In the same summer, she left and only came back the next spring. Her grandparents acted as if nothing had ever happened. They tried to ignore the "pain" till they could not. They burst out one time and started to blame each other for the reason she left. She was there too. She screamed enough was enough, he should have not hit her grandmother anymore. No one should stand for this kind of violence. He shouted at her and pointed at the gate, he kept repeating that she must get out of the house, he did not care about the fact she was a minor or whatever, he had never cared.

Her grandmother smirked and asked a rhetorical question if she had ever learned the fact yet, it was her grandmother all of those years who took care of her, in each and every aspect. Even when she got dengue at the age of nine, endured a seriously high fever that almost passed away, and had to stay in hospital for more than ten days, he did not even come to take care of her! He only came to see them once and stayed for ten minutes exactly then left!

Did she remember this? Did she notice this? She had not ever expected anything from her father and neither she did from her grandfather, as if she could sniff such a "traditional" manner and custom from the world around her where men would go on building the "nest" and women must be the ones who take care of their children. She never paid attention to this same issue until one day she realized she was becoming an ignorant child raised within the biased system. She could not say exactly what and how a woman could endure such hardship, however, her grandmother was exemplified as one to the unfair situation.

Her grandmother had to go to the market most of the day every day. She mounted a small kiosk on her own that could be moved from time to time to different spots in the local market. Due to the fact that the small kiosk was a place combined with many wooden racks, second hand clothes, hooks and iron chains, she had to carry these heavily loaded racks that hung kilograms of second-hand clothes and hooks altogether twice a day, from home to the market and then back home.

She never understood why her grandmother had to keep going on and trying too hard, despite the fact that later on she had been already receiving monthly support from uncle H. or aunt H. She was hoping to sell a few of them for another meal and from necessary to even non-essential expenses, like a set of aluminium and glass cupboards and wardrobe to "decorate" her mood.

Her grandmother had a constant hobby in which she would collect cassette tapes and good radio which always turned out to last a few months or the longest one could stay with them for a couple of years, then all would be gone to the second-hand market. On day-off mornings or when her grandfather was not there, her grandmother would enjoy listening to her favorite albums on the radio and burning several rolls of sort of tobacco herb named Cam Le[29] mixed with industrial cigarettes. She would enjoy being there with her when her grandmother was in good "mood, and help her roll the next one or prepare lunch together while passing the time.

When she was little, sometimes she would follow her grandmother to the small kiosk close to Con market[30], where she prepared a rest seat super nice and comfortable even under thirty-four-degree sunlight. She let her wander around the same area where the central market was just five minutes walk away. They would walk home together, her grandmother would hold her hand on one side, and in another hand would be a plastic basket that contained a whole world of every little necessary

---

29 A region which used to be famous with its specialty tobacco herb called after the same name, belonging to Da Nang city.
30 This central market is the largest retail and whole sale market in Da Nang.

things, from a "gamelle" or "ca men" in French-Vietnamized pronunciation – a sort of *inox* mess kit, tea towel, teapot then a one-litre thermos, oranges and endless other stuff, as if every day was a little picnic to her until she had to go to school instead.

There were summers they went to the beach near home together, no matter how the weather would be. One late afternoon, her grandmother had to close the kiosk earlier when she realized it was futile waiting for customers if the rain came. By the time she arrived home, the thick heavy cloudy sky was about to transform itself on Earth yet it did not stop them from enjoying the beautiful hidden east coast. It was the first time she had it captured, the mysterious beauty of nature entering the landscape of an observer like her. At the magical moment, there was nothing as calm as the rain by the summer sea while every single drop tapping from the sand down to the water surface, one then two then an infinity of them. They both got wet and had a lot of fun when suddenly the rain stopped, and opened to a magnificent clear sky with a glorious rainbow above their cheerful heads.

Despite those beautiful moments, they had a constant emotional conflict at least from her side. Her grandmother expected her, somehow to become one like her. She felt unfair that she had to be the only one who "broke her neck" and then went home to start cleaning after people who had done "nothing" for her. From there her grandmother kept repeating the same insults to her as the ungrateful one, the helpless, the unruly, and disobedient one and it could go on and on every single day. At those ages, she was hurt tremendously by words. She began to coil up the verbal violence to her complex mental status, and take it for granted. It became even more tricky when one day, she saw her grandmother bursting into tears while crouching toward a pile of dirty dishes, complaining and crying about why she had to do everything even after a hard day at work.

She said to her grandmother that she would do the dish after studying as she thought that it was not an urgent matter. Her grandmother would scream at her for talking back, and started to point out that she was following her grandfather's footsteps. Then her grandparents would fall into endless quarrels sporadically until late at night.

She was confused, she felt bad and sad for her grandmother, and then she felt sad for herself. She vowed to herself that she would not do anything to come across her anger ever again. She would go wash the dish at the exact time she would like her to do it. She would go complete any assigned tasks and be as silent as possible, and it would just bring them further distance from each other. It was too late.

The sorrow has been absorbing through one's inner world ever since now taking refuge in a vast quiet lake. She did not realize that she became an introvert because she felt more insecure exposing herself to anyone, yet none of them listened anyway. Her younger adolescent days were tough and so eventually was her mindset. Notwithstanding this toughness would mute any noise and ignore the injured inner child in her. One day, at that unpredicted moment, she found this other injured inner child from her grandfather.

She looked into his eyes when he shouted at her those words and replied, certainly she would be "happy" to leave this house which was nothing but a hell to anyone who lived within it. She was so sure that it made him realize – she could and she would. Right at the moment she was about to walk away, he caught her wrist and begged, "don't go. I am so sorry, just stay." And he started to cry like a little kid in front of them both.

She saw the astonished expression on her grandmother's face. Even under the toughest situations in the family, no one had ever seen him cry like that. She asked worriedly if he had any pain and needed to go to the hospital. He shook his head slightly and kept crying on her shoulder. Since that very moment, she knew for a fact that after all those years, even though they had not said any special loving words to each other yet she and her grandfather were exchanging a truly unique connection.

She did not imagine it when she cried to herself for the first time, and vowed to write about him one day after listening to his life story. She felt bad for him as no one was there with him when he was a kid as she felt bad for herself. However, she never asked him whether he had felt for her in the same position he used to experience. Because she knew he did give her unspeakable care, if not saying much more special than the way he treated other grandchildren.

It was her second year in high school and more than that, it was the worst year yet as well the best year of her adolescence.

XII.

The sleepless nights

Indeed the summer she turned seventeenth was an unforgettable one. She had quite a lot of fun time with her classmates, especially two of them, T. and X. She did not have to work at the Italian restaurant anymore as she has figured out a better part-time job as she could teach French to one of her cousins as she was ahead of him at grade twelfth and he was at the first year. She had less stress in studying as gradually changed her mindset about life after the period of being self-harmful to both her mental and physical health. And most of all, she felt better going home and spending time at home. As if the nightmare was ending and finally one could walk toward like a happy ending fairy tale.

She registered in a basketball club and would go to practice three times a week in early summer mornings. Then in the afternoon, she started to go running by the beach as she found out it was helping her migraine situation.

When she entered the last year of high school, her cousin started her second year and by that time she was already owning a Blackberry with a full QWERTY keyboard[31] yet one could touch the screen, take a picture with way "better"[32] quality and it was the thinnest BlackBerry available in the market.

She told her it was the secondhand one passed down to her from a cousin on her paternal side. She got used to knowing what other people owned while she could not since she got into that advanced high school. However, the teenage part in her telling her that she was really in need of one proper phone so as to study and keep in touch with everyone. Yet somehow her grandfather knew she needed a phone after hearing their conversation. It was a small house and one never had enough privacy to cover a secret.

Indeed she was still a teenager and she always had what she wanted if she really wanted it. She started to save her little teaching salary and calculated that it might take her six months by the time she could buy a phone with a QWERTY keyboard while a

---

31 A keyboard for a computer, typewriter, or other device that has the standard English-language key arrangement that begins with the letters Q -W - E - R - T - Y, reading from left to right across the top row.
32 Comparing with the spoken timing.

BlackBerry would take her from one year to one year and a half to finally get it. She would graduate from high school and enter university for a while by then... One day her grandfather suggested helping her with the rest of the money she needed. She was surprised by this gesture from him. She kept rejecting it because she knew he needed the money more than she did. She would ask him to save it in an emergency case instead. Her grandfather insisted on giving one million dongs[33] to her. He convinced her by saying that he still got three million dongs left for the savings. She finally agreed but was repeating she would pay him back a little every month. The fact was she never had a chance to do it.

Not long after that, on a fine chill day in the midst of the rainy season, her grandfather told her to call aunt Lo. as he could not stand for the pain anymore and they must bring him to the hospital. It was a couple of days after uncle L. informed the family that he was running for a huge debt payment and he must

---

33 About 47$ at the time.

pay it as soon as possible. He was betting in a gambling system relating to football matches.

While her grandmother agreed to sell half of their house, her grandfather definitely disagreed. They told him that he was selfish and egomaniac, narcissistic, and even when he almost died, still only put his interest as his priority – she could recall these words clearly from her grandmother. She was never sure about how her family came up with the final solution. Who did agree and who did not... In the course of the next three months, the house was sold in half to a relative of aunt H.'s husband. They paid for it quite cheaply compared with the market floor price as they knew the uncle was in need of the money, and they could pay all at once in cash.

She was the only one who stayed with him in the hospital for the first night. No one was able to do it, even the uncle who took half of their house away. They were all tired and exhausted with their own family matters, she guessed. Notwithstanding, she had to go to class the next early morning and she was exhausted too after the whole day of studying and working, she felt like her grandfather needed her to be there during this period. She heard her grandfather murmuring once every while through that night, he was still half in his consciousness half sleeping while the anaesthetic was in effect. The most tricky part was to lift him up from his position to a urine pot right by the bed. However, several times on the first night, he insisted to go to the bathroom as the urine pot became useless. She had to carry his wobbly body while trying to walk stable, carefully bring him to the loo then he told her that he could do the rest... But then in the end, he had to call her to pull his pants back as he could no longer have any strength. She could feel the weight of his body and the pain he carried while almost crawling difficulty by her side. She was just a little girl after all, she cursed, and physically she could not carry anyone even when she wanted to.

When the clock turned toward five am, he asked her to call aunt H. so he could talk with her. At the time he had already taken a rest and felt better. He told her to go home and prepare for the next day's class. It was one of the last few times he was able to speak with clear consciousness.

In the next spring, he was sent back home after two months of staying in the hospital. They finally took the other kidney which was almost "rotten" in his body. They had to bring him to another public hospital after the first month of observing and diagnosis. In addition, after three weeks length, it was crucial to proceed with a bone marrow transplant surgery. By the time he arrived at the new "house", he could no longer realize where he was...

On one of those nights when she had to stay up studying late till two or three am, she could hear his breath rhythm changing from slow to short and abruptly swift from downstairs. No one including uncle D. who had dropped his job in Saigon, and stayed all the time in the hospital with her grandfather in those long hauling three months, could hear his sudden and strange breath. She ran down carefully so she could avoid awakening anyone unnecessarily. She entered the room, and saw him then lying on a new stiff large bed in a barren room that hung in the typical concrete air from new construction, yet he did not respond to any of these details. The bouquet of vividly colorful and quiet carnations she bought the day before became even more "alive" in the scene. She felt scared and quietly cried, so she held his hand and started to pray. His retinas seemed like being covered by a dying opaque sheer yet his eye movement could show that he was trying to look forward to where she sat. He sighed and closed his eyes. He started to breathe more calmly and gradually fell back to sleep.

She never told this event to anyone as she realized that was his last night on Earth with them.

XIII.

Back to Hue province

She saw him driving a Honda Cup 50cc[34], the model which his younger step-brother had for many years. He was dressing well as she could recognize his favorite pale grey wool cotton pants and a short sleeve white silky cotton shirt. He was also wearing one of the only two pairs of black lace-up shoes he had gotten for so long and kept wearing them to any wedding events of his children. His hair was always a bit curvy, following certain lines if he let them grow further which was combed well as she remembered he would spend time doing it every morning. He was giving a cheerful smile under the sunshine and a little breeze could only make both of them feel more relaxed in his departure. They did not talk at all until she asked him where he would drive to. He kept smiling and started off the engine. When he was about to drive off to somewhere else, he said clearly "I am going to Hue."

---

34 An underbone motorcycle from the brand Honda, a Japanese multinational conglomerate Motor company, with a four-stroke single-cylinder engine ranging in displacement from 49 to 124 cc.

It was three pm on a hot late spring afternoon. She woke up among the mixed noise of people chatting, whispering, walking up and down the only staircase in the new house, the friction between the furniture and the tiled floor while someone was trying to arrange the house in a hurry. The Thursday afternoon sun hit hard yet surprisingly she no longer felt that migraine at this time of the day. The dream gave her a sudden contentment and serenity even though it might seem like a "spiritual" message between the dead and the living one, another "secret" between them as they had shared long before. Her grandfather passed away on the same morning. It was her eighteen years old birthday.

Of course, there was no birthday celebration on that day as there were none thrown since she started secondary school. But it was the eighteenth birthday – the one in which she had been waiting and "preparing" for it. There would be three things which she had to complete once she reached the age, obtaining a passport, travelling to a place she had never been, and passing university entrance exams. Instead of thinking about this bucket list, she had to pass them aside and stay helpful to the family under such situation.

On that very day, her father flew back home, but there was little exchange of conversation between them. Later, as everyone gathered around the table after a long day of receiving funeral visitors, he unexpectedly dampened her spirits, uttering cold words, "don't even think about a birthday celebration. That's out of the question now. Get rid of that silly idea from your mind." His motivation behind these words remained elusive to everyone, and it served no purpose except to inflict tremendous pain and embarrass to her. Then one of her aunts said to him to go take a rest, everybody must be tired now.

All of her uncles and aunts were there exchanging the funeral program and setup together. Her grandmother would keep talking with their neighbors and her own siblings who came to pay condolence to the family.

On the second day, D. came with her grandmother to offer incense and stay with them for a while. After that she took a long walk with D. by the beach as she gave her a little birthday card. She was almost bursting into tears yet tried to remain calm and a little stoic to the situation. D. said that they could go have ice cream anytime she felt like. As always she appreciated her best friend's presence in her life even until some points later she was not sure whether D. kept seeing her as a best friend in life. Because for many years on she would fly away from Danang, and remained silent then one day she would pop up and call D. They would meet and D. would drive her around the city, walk along the river bank and keep talking like the old days despite the fact that they had not witnessed many important events in each other's life later on.

The funeral lasted almost one week as it certainly had many people coming over and offering condolences. In many ways, he was not only a well-known tailor yet had also got the infamy for being in a violent and adultery situation with his wife for several years. However, most of the people who came to visit the funeral gave him more respect than hatred. Indeed he was a respectful man in other aspects. He was charming, they would say. He always spoke well and had a decent manner. Despite the fact that her grandmother would always disagree about all of these, and carry such a bitter loathsome to him with her forever.

Finally, two strange men who represented her family, and belonged to the funeral assistance crew with their utmost meticulous gesture and skill, came to seal the coffin. It was Hue as she could have come to the clue earlier due to the fact she was not a spiritual one in mind. As time goes by, there are many things in the world that one could not explain thoroughly even under scientific eyes, and somehow holding one end of a spiritual explanation might save one's soul from restless nights.
She did not feel the difference between the dead and the living until she saw them attentively placing the radiant veneer box under the ground through thick ropes and a firm pillar system, after preparing a long-hour befitting ritual and a good decent excavation. As if those bottled-up feelings and tragic events had been buried with him, she felt such a sudden relief, and at the same time, a deep nostalgia for whatever had happened during those years they shared together.

She said to no one and turned to no one. She helped him keep them secrets as long as she could and realized that having she talked about it with someone, might not make her less than a benefactor of the secret keeper. However, it was not everything.

Excruciatingly she found out the fact that there might be many details in the story which were made up. As amusing as it might go, the whole story about the escaping boy did not start until he was fourteen years old, as his younger step brother confirmed this.

However, she could recall some moments when both of the step-brothers went on a quarrel about at what age those events might have happened. Her grandfather insisted that the other brother did not have any clue what was happening, by pointing out the fact that he had carried him as a little baby on his back or by the hip, back and forth between home and a local school.

She could not sleep well for the last two nights in Saigon. It was the second time back home after the 2020 pandemic. She was trying her best to be balanced between her, "herself" and "nothingness." The "her" that everybody sees as who she might be, the "herself" as she thought that was supposedly her, and the "nothingness" in respect of letting go of all of these definitions. She realized that none of these definitions really matter as she simply did not walk those paths.

When she closed her eyes, everything was floating by and she could hear that random music from the neighbor's coffee shop, the jovial "freedom" scream from one's lung, doves cuckooing over the old house' rooftop every dry season morning, the quietness from one's vast melancholy, and the past is all what she might see in such moments.

Memory, after all, is a fragmental remaining product of what we perceive from the past. And every time we press the "replay" button, the feeling might sound the same but somewhat the fact would be played like an old cassette mix-tape. We could find the end song from the beginning of a playlist then this very same end song would keep repeating after every two or three other new songs as if the tape had been spelled to jumpstart through time. Memory will quickly come back yet fact may be long gone.

Nevertheless there exists this kind of pictorial memory where one could capture graphically every single sense within the same picture frame. It was just like a yesterday event, she was still an innocent little girl hanging around the old house, asking him a thousand non-sense questions about what he was doing, if he could let her play with the rearing part of a tapestry or a piece of fabric after being cut to tailor which would be omitted anyway, if he would show her how to tailor too, bargaining her end for not taking nap or getting rebuke by leaving home to hang out with the neighbors without saying any words, or even asking. Those days were simply perfect, and because of that, they were beautiful.

There are countless momentary memories encountered in the present feelings in which one sees that they had happened before. And such a paradox is that after only a few years living off the country home, one would have to buy into such a normalcy and fantasy blend – a stranger from one's own country, yet one would hardly ever become a stranger to one's own memory landscape.

Short Story

The Well

I.

Well, I grew up most of my childhood with my grandparents in a beach city sixteen hours by train from Ho Chi Minh city. I was lucky to be in touch with the ocean right from that time regardless of the fact that I had not been taken care of by an "ordinary" family, yet sometimes I wonder what it would be different though.

Back then we moved back and forth between two places by train, we just took advantage of the powerful technology world for a few years recently. I guess you might be surprised by some actual aspects that Vietnam is still a developing country, and we have just launched and officially inaugurated our very first subway system around the end of 2019, yet new flight route operations and plane delays are both something quite usual to us. Even so, the wealthy class still drive supercars, stay at a five-star hotel for meetings, dress up with Louis Vuitton, and travel to Europe once every while easily as if ordering a pizza from home at five am is such a possible thing in Vietnam.

I am not writing these words to complain about this fun fact or to satisfy my craving for such things. I do not have a luxurious life in Europe and neither wish to, and from what I see, most of everyone stays humble here and anywhere I have traveled in this continent. Not every day I can see a "nicely shaped" woman with fancy clothes stepping out from a Lamborghini, and that must be another dimension of life where one could have a thing or two to do with Hollywood influence by evoking such an "absurd" moment on Earth. Of course, I have changed quite an awful deal in seeing the world since I have been living here in one of the busiest cities in Europe.

I was thinking about mundane tasks we humans get to complete in our life while taking a quick shower after a late afternoon nap. I usually do not have a habit of napping but one could never know what will happen during the day going on. I let the hot water pour out all over my body then started rubbing soap from shoulders to arms and suddenly it dropped out of my hand with its very sloppy nature, creating a thud loudly against the bottom of the bathtub, sliding through the weak stream running from the shower. In a blink of an eye, I saw myself picturing an old memory of when I was still living with my grandparents in the old house where they had not taken down the well yet.

A well was a common spot either in the old house structure or every ancient village and scarcely in a few alleys in big cities. They used to represent a part of the culture and scenery in Vietnam, especially in the countryside. Each house must build a well as the "fountain of life" because almost every activity involved around it, from washing dishes and doing laundry to taking showers (for both men and women, children and old people, pets, etc), from cleaning furniture to washing off mud and dust from fresh vegetables or fruits, from main domestic tasks to just playing with water by kids like us.

Our house was not as huge as I could remember by now and neither we had a second floor with an attic but the most memorable part of its construction was how open and cozy it was, and that how it helped us record memories from daily living. Along the right side of the house, there was a narrow roofless alley where we used to hang clothes on sunny or even just dry days which we called a piece of simple luck through typical rainy seasons.

The house did not last that long even though I was living there for more than ten years. We got to offer half of the house in order to earn an amount of money in the short term and pay off the debt of my uncle.

Back to the well, it stayed right at the end of the small alley which we called the bathroom, simply surrounded by the main walls and covered by a small aluminum sheet with a wooden frame door that actually led to the main part of the house. Once you do not need your privacy, hang the door by the wall, and it would become a common washing room for everybody. For example of a casual day, my aunt would have been doing the laundry by the well while

I was brushing my teeth and washing my face beside her, and my grandmother was cleaning fresh tea leaves in a stainless steel sink on the other side (this small space actually was connected to the alley as well other parts of the house, ended up having more than one door on one's end and a large window on one side) to begin her working day with homemade tea and sprinkled ginger.

Right there at the center of our everyday activities was the existence of the well. The very familiar one that was captured lively in every memory during my growth until I was eighteen years old. It was the best time of all as much as the worst of all. I turned eighteen just on the day my grandfather passed away.

Before that, the well was knocked down in the same year in order to separate the house into neat and exact halfness of each end. We took the side where the well was obviously, and from there we built up a new house with two stories and a balcony where every summer afternoon the heat was a terrible torture of staying up there around thirty-eight Celcius degrees, and for quite some time it kept being hotter every single year. I remember we did all the possible ways to prevent the heat from such intensive sunny afternoons but as long as it is summer, the weather will be scorching and humid or roasting hot again.

The moment the soap fell down to my foot, there was an old reaction I did not think that I might have been keeping with me for such a long time. I was afraid of losing the soap to fall into the well as it had been a very big deal to us back then. Once someone, anyone, was careless or just on an unlucky day that had their hands slipping a soap to the well, that one definitely had to" work" hard and patiently in order to bring "the strange object" out of the well right on the same day, otherwise it could cause a messy chemical "pollution" to the water. Meaning then we could not clean fresh ingredients for cooking nor process a "proper" hygiene routine. As we cooked every day for every single meal, we prepared new dishes as we had five people at that time, my grandparents, two aunts and me, hence saving clean water had been educated and shaped within our conscience.

II.

There is one more thing I need to explain to you that even up to 2002, we still kept up consuming potable water from our neighbor, and we paid every single liter we bought from them. They were a better-condition family who owned a large and wide house with a vast garden right by our house's left side to almost the end of the alley. They ran a little farm by raising a kind of quail that later on would produce rack and rack of eggs. The business was good but soon as the old mother decided to divide the house into four parts, two for sale, one for her son, and the last part where it was originally the taro[35] garden, she stayed there alone until she passed away just a few years after my grandfather's death.

Water is always an important part of our life one way or another even after stopping to purchase it from the neighbor. We set up our own potable water

---

35 Taro is a root vegetable, a food staple in African, South Asia, East Asia South East Asia, Oceanic culture.

system with a parameter clock under the ground within the front yard. Our grandparents had certain rules of not wasting water due to only one main reason, for being able to pay an economic bill each month. That was why we always treasured the existence of the well and its miraculous natural line of water. Such a pity that we could not keep it with us by now and then. To mention it here, I miss the feeling of showering under the fresh cool water during endless hot summer days as well as those accidental moments, when someone happened to slip off soap or anything else, be it a stainless steel spoon or a plastic water scoop.

I remember there was a summer night, I followed my aunt sneakily to her friend's house but later I changed my mind, and instead stopped by my friend's house right at the same alley where my house is which we still share such common nowadays. When you are back from "traveling" too far for too long from your childhood, you recognize that even the same alley, people, atmosphere, and the very typical kind of old beautiful vibe can not keep things staying in the same way they used to be.

Of course, my grandfather is no longer there to threaten me not to leave home without any adult's permission in the house, and I have made my home so far from the well...

I came home around an hour later meanwhile my aunt was already back from her friend's house. The fact that we were supposed to have dinner around 8 pm and I just appeared all of a sudden around 9 pm without even considering what might have happened to me then. It was clear and straight that my grandfather was extremely furious at me and my impulsive absence. He held a wooden ruler in his hand, the type that was used for measuring fabric and hence made specifically for tailors. He was a tailor, a good one, and famous as well for a while. Waving the ruler in the air, he pointed it at me, and warned me again not to do things based on my own interests.

These kinds of house rules went throughout my childhood and left a seriously powerful influence which I managed to get over. Once I began my adolescence and got to become a young adult right after his "absence" in life, I stopped responding to this kind of "threat". There were many times when we argued and he forbade me to do something. I used to cry quite easily in such situations, yet I could not cry in front of people during his funeral.

Later on, the following day, I discovered that my grandparents were so worried about my absence that they called my father who was living in Ho Chi Minh city, and started to do some serious research around the house and the area. My grandfather even tried to bail as much water out of the well as possible so he could climb down and take a "look" at whether I, unfortunately, had slipped over the cement floor and fallen into it. The power was accidentally off during the time I was not at home, adding up to the overall thrilling atmosphere, evoking such a scared scenario.

Things always turn out to be worse in our minds once we are worried and not capable of knowing what we desperately want to know. The worst part of the story stayed at the electricity break in the area. Both of my grandparents were extremely nervous that they decided to set up the research into the well under such pale light from candles which she held for lighting his steps, and once every while the wax simply melt and reluctantly fell on my grandfather's white T-shirt shoulder, the kind which used to be his favorite homey cloth, and poor the old soul, this hot melting candle felt on his hair as well.

I felt a guilty statement rolling up and down my stomach, I did not know that was love then. I am always late to such things, even now my reactions to events and strokes of emotion come in a very late manner. Even if I do not feel anything at the same moment, it does not mean that I do not have responsibility for my present feeling and attitude. Because I have always been aware about my responsibility.

The fact that bar soap contains fewer chemical components that may be harmful to the quality of water and sewage systems, and becomes the most self-sustainable option for the environment, has always been my lifestyle compass.

As the retrospective streams a little further, I recalled that there was a period of a whole year in which I did not use hair shampoo at all. I was just an ordinary fourteen-year-old girl, trying to save the environment when acknowledging that the annual temperature rise may damage our existence on Earth by making the decision of hair shampoo withdrawal for a year. By reducing the chemical as well as oil and plastic waste into water, we can simply help treat it a little easier in the process.

What happened? I have had to use hair shampoo again which contains mainly herbal and natural ingredients, for the truth that my hair was turning into a stiff and dry straw "swab". Nevertheless, I keep going on using bar soap for body and hand washing since then.

I picked up the soap, and inadvertently released a grin at the way that childhood memory could evoke such nostalgia. At that moment I knew I will keep carrying them on in my life and maybe someday, I will tell my children a thousand and one stories about the well in my childhood.

Here I am again, trying to follow the passage of time and events, connect every single one my grandfather had ever told me, and write them down. I am certain that in some way this book can not cover the depth of each story landscape I have ever experienced and witnessed. However, I did make a vow to myself that one day I would write about him and for him as a little present to him. And to all of us, especially those who have been victims of family violence, depression, and anyone who has ever felt lost in life.

A Memoir by Chi Jade Tran

Edited by Chi Jade Tran

Cover Designed by Huong Anh Trinh

Printed in Poland
by Amazon Fulfillment
Poland Sp. z o.o., Wrocław
31 August 2023

d60411f3-47ca-41c7-a26a-ebce4fdd2b47R01